The Pressures of Life

Longman Imprint Books
General Editor: Michael Marland

Companion cassettes, with readings of some of the key stories,
are available for the following:
The Leaping Lad and other stories
The Human Element
A Sillitoe Selection
Late Night on Watling Street
A Casual Acquaintance
Loves, Hopes, and Fears

LONGMAN IMPRINT BOOKS

The Pressures of Life

four television plays by

Richard Harris
Barry Hines
Julia Jones
Michael O'Neill and Jeremy Seabrook

selected and edited by
Michael Marland BA

Headmaster, Woodberry Down Comprehensive School,
London

with questions for discussion and writing by
Chris Buckton

Thames Television have mounted new productions of
Barry Hines' *Speech Day* and Julia Jones' *The Piano*
for transmission throughout the country as part of
the ITV schools' series *The English Programme.*

Longman

LONGMAN GROUP LIMITED
London
*Associated companies branches and representatives
throughout the world*

This edition first published 1977

ISBN 0 582 23329 1

Printed in Great Britain by Whitstable Litho Ltd., Whitstable.

Contents

The Pressures of Life

Sometimes we feel that we are on top of life—able to follow our interests, succeed in our work, get on well with other people, and everything goes smoothly. At other times, we feel frustrated—we cannot quite manage what is needed; we seem to hit problems that are beyond us; we feel overcome by "the pressures of life". These four plays all show people of today suffering in one way or another from the pressures of life today. The plays are by different authors, and were written for different series, but they each have "the pressures of life" in common, and in each we meet characters who are having difficulty coping.

Short plays on television are one of the most popular and probably one of the best art forms of today. The television screen has encouraged a form of realistic, compressed, and popular drama which explores contemporary characters in contemporary settings. The best of these have a depth of understanding of human nature and the predicaments that people get into that makes the play seem more than just a typical problem of the moment. Neil's conflict with Fred Pooley in the first play, for instance, makes us think about the ways in which people's pride and their prejudices affect their relationship with others. These are, above all, plays about people, people pushing against their surroundings and fighting the pressures of life.

The atmosphere of each play is different, and the reader should try to imagine the background of each. *Speech Day* depends on the atmosphere of an old-fashioned school building, just as *A Right Dream of Delight* depends on the cheery, bright comfort of a modern light factory, and *The Piano* on our sensing of Ada's house, which is cramped but homely and comforting. Readers can build up a picture of each setting, not only the look, but the sounds of the schoolboys singing, and the demolition machinery at work—all the details which are hinted at or described in the printed text and which the television screen would bring to life.

Each story centres on a small group of people. As the plays are *about* these people, the reader needs to have a good idea of what they are like. You can't get much of this from their looks, because in the text of a play writers do not give such full descriptions as they do in novels. (You will find that the photographs help.) Still, it is possible to get your impression from the hints in the directions, what other characters say about them, and what the main characters say themselves. Listen carefully in your mind to *how* they speak; they each have their own way of putting things, their favourite words, and special phrases.

Of course, these plays were written for performance on television, where what you *see* is as important as what you *hear*. Perhaps the reader will be able to imagine some of the scenes as they would look on a television screen—Edgar pottering around his tiny garden in *The Piano*, or the coach journey in *A Right Dream of Delight*, for instance. Look out also for the way in which the writer makes the camera jump from one scene to another, and so makes us think of the contrasts, like the factory scenes that are played over the school songs in *Speech Day*.

The pressures in these plays have wider echoes. The causes and results of what happens in these particular plays are not so very different from other people's lives. You may never, for instance, be in a situation like Neil in *Reasonable Suspicion*. But what you learn of his motives and his change of heart may connect with situations that you have known. The reader's enjoyment of the plays is increased if these wider meanings are realised. The immediate background problem of *The Piano* is the demolition of an old couple's home, but it isn't just about *that* couple, or even about the unpleasantness of demolition. The wider concern of the play is with the conflicts between different kinds of dreams about the future, and between people's personal ambitions and their responsibilities to other people.

Each of these four plays, like those in the companion volume *Conflicting Generations*, must have started with an idea in the author's mind that excited him or her, and about which the author felt strongly. If you read carefully, you will come to share this idea. You will see also that although these plays are quite separate, there are similarities and links as well as contrasts.

M.M.

Reasonable Suspicion
by Richard Harris

The Cast
Detective Sergeant Smith
Sergeant Ken Ridgeway
P.C. Harry Coombes
P.C. Fred Pooley
Maggie, *his girl friend*
Pat
Geoff
Neil
Ruth, *his girl friend*

Reasonable Suspicion
PART ONE

Outside a pub

Early Sunday evening. A small pub near the town centre. Quiet—with something to establish the "Sunday" feeling . . . the distant sound of church bells . . . or perhaps a Salvation Army band.

After a moment, the pub door opens and four people come out . . . Pooley his girlfriend Maggie . . . Geoff and Pat. All about the same age Pooley in civvies. Geoff is pocketing a half-bottle of Scotch.

We go with them as they move to where Geoff's car is parked (a Triumph 1500) . . . Geoff is feeling pretty chipper. Pooley is there under sufferance: Maggie is clearly not his most favourite lady at the moment.

Geoff unlocks the car doors. The two girls get in the back. Geoff gets behind the wheel, leans over to unlock the front passenger door. Pooley is about to get in when suddenly he stops—something away from the car has taken his attention. He leans into the car, says something to Geoff ("Hang on a minute, will you?") and moves away from the car.

The other three watch him go, not knowing quite what he's up to.

A tatty old man (not a tramp) is poking about with some boxes etc. which have been put out at the back entrance to a row of shops. Pooley is crossing the road and approaching him.

In long shot we see him reach the old man and start talking to him. They obviously know each other . . . Pooley is remonstrating with the old man who is being defensive.

Pooley brusquely seeing the old man off. He starts to shuffle away unwillingly.

Pooley is standing, watching. Geoff approaches him. As they both watch the retreating old man for a moment.

GEOFF What's it all about?

Pooley doesn't look at him, but still keeps his eye on the old man.

POOLEY (*calling*) Go on—scarper! (*A pause.*) Poor old devil.

GEOFF What's he done?

POOLEY Nothing—yet. (*A moment.*) No . . . it's pathetic . . . one of these old fellahs, no family, living in a tatty little room . . . spends most of his time walking around the town, poking about in dustbins— God knows what for.

GEOFF Not exactly what you might call upsetting anyone . . .

POOLEY (*with an edge to his voice*) In a couple of hours he'll be drunk out of his mind, chucking punches at whoever comes in handy. We have him in about once a fortnight. I told him to go home and behave himself. (*A flat smile.*) That's all.

He turns and moves back towards the car. Geoff permits himself a little smile and then goes after him. They return to the car and drive off.

Maggie's sitting room

The small sitting room of a furnished flat rented by Maggie.

Pooley, Geoff and Pat. Geoff—who is very slightly drunk—is having what he fondly believes to be a "discussion" with Pooley. Pat is rather embarrassed. Pooley is fed up but up to now has just about maintained his cool. There is a positive atmosphere then, as we go straight in with:

POOLEY . . . Look—there's bound to be friction in my job . . .

GEOFF . . . that's all I'm saying . . .

POOLEY . . . all right—yeah.

GEOFF . . . right. So . . .

PAT . . . oh for goodness sake, Geoff—shut up . . .

GEOFF . . . go and help Maggie with the coffee.

PAT Don't start giving me orders.

GEOFF (*grimace at Pooley*) Women's Lib.

Pat looks at Pooley who—always the ladies' man—gives her a comforting smile.

PAT Only happy when he's arguing.

GEOFF Not arguing, sweetheart—discussing.

PAT With you it's the same thing.

GEOFF (*leans into her*) It's called having an enquiring mind.

PAT It's called a pain in the neck.

She gets up and moves to the door.

GEOFF Get to the kitchen where you belong, woman.

PAT (*looks at him*) Your mother's got a lot to answer for.

She goes out. Geoff smiles flatly at Pooley.

4

GEOFF Marry her?

POOLEY Little cracker if you ask me.

GEOFF (*taps his head*) It's here, mate—here.

He grimaces, leans forward, takes up the half-bottle of Scotch, indicates it to Pooley.

GEOFF No, no—you're on—whaddya call it?—night duty.
My mistake, constable.

As he pours himself a shot of whisky, Pooley shifts uncomfortably in his chair and glances at his watch.

Maggie's kitchen

It is simply a corner, maybe a kitchen-cum-bathroom. Maggie is making four cups of Nescafé. Pat is with her. A pause.

PAT Sorry.

Maggie looks at her. Pat indicates the sitting room.

MAGGIE (*smiles*) Makes a change from football. (*With a mixture of amusement.*) Poor Fred.

The sitting room

POOLEY You should try my job—just try it—you'd find out.

GEOFF . . . not my scene.

POOLEY . . . well it's bloody mine. And I do it the way I know how.

GEOFF Which is precisely my point. You've been conditioned—by the system.

POOLEY I've been what?

GEOFF . . . you pay a certain type of man to do a certain type of job and when he does it the way he knows how—the way the system makes him—you complain that he's overstepping the mark. . . .

PAT What do you mean—certain type of man?

During this, the two girls have entered and distributed coffee. Maggie manages a smile at Pooley who still isn't having any.

GEOFF He knows what I mean—don't you, constable?

POOLEY Knock off this "constable" bit, will you . . . ?

PAT (*to Geoff*) . . . you know your trouble, don't you? You're a snob.

GEOFF (*to Maggie*) And to think that fifty years ago the working classes could neither read nor write . . .

POOLEY (*a half-grin*) Snob?

He hasn't really understood but the inference has got through.

GEOFF I don't condone it, but I understand . . .

PAT . . . understands everybody, does Geoffrey. Especially the workers. Oh yes. You should have heard him when the power strike was on . . . very understanding then, he was . . .

GEOFF He knows what I mean . . .

PAT You would have made a good copper.

GEOFF Can you imagine?

PAT Yes I bloody can. You're so damned pompous.

GEOFF She's annoyed. Always swears when she's annoyed.

He grins, takes up his cup, drinks with little finger deliberately extended, ladylike.

MAGGIE What time are you on, Fred?

POOLEY Ten o'clock.

MAGGIE Oh.

She smiles. He pointedly looks at his watch, making it quite clear that there are better ways of spending their time.

GEOFF You know one of the biggest troubles, don't you?

The following three lines of dialogue cut through Geoff's next speech, so that he ploughs on regardless through them.

PAT Oh God, you're not starting again. Where's my coat, Maggie?

MAGGIE . . . I'll fetch it . . .

PAT (*to Geoff*) Come on—we're going . . .

The two girls go out of the room.

GEOFF . . . the car. Most people drive a car—right? Which means that most of us are potential law-breakers. Wouldn't you say—I mean, from experience—that 99 times out of a hundred—when the ordinary man-in-the-street comes in contact—direct contact—with the police—it's something to do with his car. Either he's speeding . . . or it's been stolen . . . or the breath-alyser . . .

The two girls—Pat now wearing her topcoat and carrying Geoff's topcoat—have entered.

PAT (*interrupting him*) Are you coming or what?

POOLEY . . . look. I'm a copper. I do my job. That's all.

GEOFF Don't be so defensive.

He knocks back his coffee, stands, and gets into his topcoat aided by Pat.

POOLEY . . . this is my one night off. I came here to see my girlfriend . . .

PAT . . . we shouldn't have stayed . . .

MAGGIE . . . don't be silly, Pat . . .

POOLEY Oh—great—thanks.

GEOFF I'm interested, that's all.

POOLEY What do you do?

GEOFF Ah!

POOLEY No—come on—what do you do?

PAT He works in an architect's office.

6

POOLEY Do you? Well my sister's just moved into a new house and the ceiling's falling down.

GEOFF Builder—not architect. (*Pooley grimaces.*) I'm interested . . . I'm trying to find out what makes you tick . . .

POOLEY . . . makes me what?

MAGGIE ("*lightly*") . . . oh come on now, Geoff . . .

GEOFF . . . not just you—the law.

PAT Oh God—look—it's late . . .

POOLEY . . . why I joined?

PAT . . . will you please come . . .

POOLEY . . . why do you work in a builder's office?

GEOFF . . . architect.

PAT . . . because his father got him the job.

GEOFF . . . because I'm interested and because I've got the qualifications.

POOLEY Right.

GEOFF Right: so what are you qualifications?

POOLEY I'm a sod?

GEOFF (*Geoff has got exactly what he's been angling for.*)
I'll remember to stay out of your way then.

POOLEY I would if I were you: you're just about my mark.

GEOFF Now you're getting nasty.

POOLEY That's right.
A moment. Very uneasy. Then:

PAT Goodnight.
She tries a smile at Pooley; then looks at Geoff.
The two girls exit.

GEOFF No offence.

POOLEY Just—leave it alone, will you?

GEOFF (*Geoff moves to the door, but . . . with a deliberately "drunken" slur*)
Incidentally, I'm not driving, ossifer . . . she is . . .
He grins and goes out. Pooley, left alone, simmers. He moves around. Maggie enters.

POOLEY Come round, she says . . . we'll have a nice quiet evening . . .

MAGGIE I didn't know they were coming . . .

POOLEY I should bloody hope not.

MAGGIE I haven't seen Pat for ages.

POOLEY Well you certainly made up for it.

MAGGIE I said I'm sorry . . .

POOLEY . . . what the hell does she see in him?

MAGGIE I think she's beginning to wonder.

POOLEY . . . bloody looking down his nose at me . . .

MAGGIE . . . he wasn't . . .

POOLEY . . . as soon as they found out . . . you can see the look on their faces . . . if I'd have been an engineer or something—that would have been it—end of conversation. But no: I'm a copper. What makes me tick.

Maggie takes up the cups. Goes out. Pooley sits, fuming.

The kitchen

Maggie putting the crockery in the sink. She turns to see Pooley in the doorway.

POOLEY Sorry.

A moment. Then she smiles and moves to put her arms around him. He puts his arms round her.

MAGGIE Daft, that's what you are.

POOLEY I get fed up with it, that's all.

MAGGIE You know . . . for someone who gives out that he's so sure of himself . . . you really get touchy, don't you?

POOLEY I get fed up with defending what I do for a living.

MAGGIE You know it was the uniform I fancied, don't you? You came a very poor second.

POOLEY *(grins)* Lot of birds fancy me in that uniform.

MAGGIE There you are—you love it—you know you do.

POOLEY A living—that's all it is—a living. I'd chuck it in tomorrow.

MAGGIE If what?

POOLEY According to him . . . if I had the brains.

The Station Office

Coombes is working at the desk. He looks up as Pooley—still in civvies—comes in through the main entrance.

COOMBES You're cutting it fine.

POOLEY Don't you start. *(But grins.)* Scored, didn't I?

He makes to move on. Coombes gets on with his work.

POOLEY Harry . . . *(Coombes looks up)* Doesn't matter.

He goes on through. Coombes works. Gets up, taking a sheet of paper through.

The Sergeant's Office

Ken is using the telephone. He winks his thanks to Coombes, who puts down the paper and exits. Ken jots down car numbers, and repeats them.

KEN . . . that's it, is it? Yeah, will do. *(Remembers.)* We found that chippy's van, y'know. In the woods. *(Grins.)* No . . . off the path, hundred yards into the trees, not a scratch on it. Smithy reckons it was somebody practising for their advanced driving test—passed an' all in my book. Yeah. (*Grins.*) I'll let you know if any of this lot turns up. Cheers, Tom.

He rings off. Makes a note. Sees his hands are slightly dirty, frowns distastefully.

The washroom

Pooley, now in uniform, adjusts his tie in the mirror. Ken comes in and washes his hands.

KEN   Keep your eyes open for a blue Cortina, will you? Haven't got the number—possibly J registration—not sure of that, but anyway—dark blue Cortina, one—maybe two—passengers.

Pooley leans into the mirror and runs a hand over his hair.

POOLEY   Anything special, sarge?

KEN   You should have been a ballet dancer.

POOLEY   (*flat, serious, still examining himself*) Me dad was always saying that.

KEN   Those break-ins down the High Street. Had a bloke in—reckons he saw a Cortina taking off. Be about the right time and it fits in with the witness we got for the one last month, so keep your eyes open—he's about due for another crack.

POOLEY   Made a right mess of that last shop he did. Dead clumsy. Must be a beginner.

KEN   Beginner or not he's about three hundred quid better off; much more of it and someone'll start getting the big stick out. See him off, Pooley, and you'll be doing yourself a nice little favour.

Ken towels his hands. He assumes that Pooley will leave, but glances up to see him looking at him.

POOLEY   Can I ask you a question, sarge?

KEN   You can ask.

Slight pause.

POOLEY   How long did it take you to make sergeant?

KEN   Bit early for you to start thinking about that, isn't it?

POOLEY   . . . just—interested.

KEN   . . . I thought you were only interested in CID.

POOLEY   . . . you know . . . just in case it . . . you know . . . doesn't work out.

KEN   Five years.

Pooley nods.

KEN   Fancy a set of stripes, do you?

POOLEY   Don't fancy not having 'em. (*Slight pause.*) One of these days. Jesus . . . when I think of old Harry . . .

KEN   . . . old Harry knows more about day to day police work than any of us . . .

POOLEY   . . . yeah . . . but . . . I mean . . . it's . . . ambition.

KEN   Know all about ambition, do you, Pooley?

POOLEY   I reckon you do.

He's stepped slightly out of line and there's a faintly uneasy moment. Then Pooley exits. Ken looks at himself in the mirror, running a hand across his hair. Straightens up, continues to look at himself. What he sees, and knows he sees, is an ambitious man.

Another sitting room

Ruth's flat. Reproductions and posters, many of them "protest" posters, decorate the walls.

Ruth—about 20—is sprinkling food for fish in a small tank. But her mind is very much on Neil, who is bringing things through from the bedroom and ramming them into an elderly holdall. He is in his early 20's, works in computers, has a degree.

They've had a row. She's unwilling to continue it. He's riding it to the bitter end.

RUTH   Don't you think it's . . . well, it's just stupid driving up the motorway in the mood you're in . . . ?

NEIL   . . . I thought you'd finished.

RUTH   . . . if you're trying to worry me—all right—you're succeeding . . .

NEIL   I don't—bloody—care. (*He's fussing just that bit too much with the holdall.*)

RUTH   It's the same every time you go away . . . you have to start a row . . . why do you do it, Neil? What are you trying to prove—how independent you are . . . ?

NEIL   Can't you see anything? You get on my nerves.

RUTH   Go to hell then.

Satisfied now, he collects his cigarettes and lighter from a table, shoves them in his pocket, exits, and reappears pulling on a rather shabby raincoat.

RUTH   It's gone eleven . . . you'll arrive there in the middle of the night and be half-asleep all day. You said this meeting was important. If you want to go on sulking . . . at least . . . sulk on the sofa for the night . . .

NEIL   (*He has already got the coat on and is taking up the holdall.*) I'll collect my things when I get back.

RUTH   Go to hell.

He smiles flatly and goes out. We see Ruth in close-up for a moment, before cutting to a panda car moving through the main town area, which is deserted and quiet.

Inside the panda car

Pooley is driving. He is unwrapping a stick of chewing gum. He puts it in his mouth and chews mechanically. As he drives, he is glancing out of the side window. Suddenly his attention hardens.

The panda car quietly pulls to a stop outside a row of shops which includes a jeweller's . . . and just past a side turning.

The street

Pooley gets out of the car, closing the door quietly. He holds his torch, checks the stick in his pocket, spits out the gum.

Pooley approaches the corner of the side street. He stops, discreetly in the shadows. The camera follows his gaze, and we see parked some way down this side street—more or less level with the back of the shops—a dark grey Cortina, lights out, parked tail towards the High Street. We can just make out the shape of someone sitting behind the wheel.

Close up of Pooley, as he stands in the shadows, watching.

Again we cut back to the car, then, slowly tracking . . . as Pooley moves quietly towards it. Now we can see the definite shape of a man at the wheel. The registration number—which ends in a "J".

The camera continues slowly tracking as he leaves the pavement so that he approaches the car from the driver's side. Comes right up to the driver's window. The man at the wheel clearly hasn't seen or heard him. Then he suddenly becomes aware and looks up.

Cut to another angle. We see the man at the wheel is Neil. He wears the raincoat and a pair of gloves. His first reaction is one of slight shock . . . then that vague shift towards guilt that most of us get when confronted by a copper. After a pause he unwinds the window and looks up at Pooley.

NEIL Yes?

POOLEY What you doing here then?

NEIL I beg your pardon?

He had understood perfectly well. It's that resentment of authority: the first twig on the fire.

POOLEY It's half past twelve—I said what are you doing here?

NEIL I'm thinking.

POOLEY Thinking?

NEIL That's right—thinking. Some of us do it, you know.

Pooley flashes his torch at the tax disc.

POOLEY Your car, is it?

NEIL *(a heavy sigh)* Yes.

POOLEY D'you mind telling me the number?

NEIL G . . . *(But stops. He's genuinely forgotten.)* . . . look . . . it's my car . . .

11

POOLEY Where was it taxed?

NEIL Northampton.

POOLEY Says here Hertford.

NEIL (*"patiently"*) It's a secondhand car—I've only had it a month— I've forgotten the number—I'm sorry.

POOLEY Let's have a look at your licence then. (*After a pause Neil digs into his wallet.*) And your insurance if you've got it.

NEIL All here—officer.
He passes the licence and cover note to Pooley. Pooley examines it— irritatingly slowly—in the light of the torch.

POOLEY Neil Edward Yeldham.

NEIL (*spelling it*) Y-E-L-D-H-A-M. (*Pooley hands back the documents, with a flat smile.*) All right?

POOLEY Cold, are you?

NEIL What?

POOLEY (*nods towards*) Gloves.

NEIL I always wear gloves when I drive.
Pooley shines his torch into the back of the car.
In the light of the torch, we see the elderly holdall on the floor behind the front seats. On the back seat, a large rubber torch.

POOLEY Where've you been?

NEIL Oh now look—come on . . .

POOLEY What are you doing here?

NEIL I don't see . . .

POOLEY . . . what's in the bag?

NEIL What bag?

POOLEY You heard.

NEIL None of your business.

POOLEY I'm making it my business.

NEIL Look—you're not dealing with some tuppeny-ha'penny little halfwit now, you know . . .

POOLEY . . . I'm asking you what's in the bag . . .

NEIL . . . who the hell d'you think you are . . . ?

POOLEY . . . all right—let's have you out . . .

NEIL . . . tinpot bloody Hitler . . .

POOLEY . . . out. (*He opens the driver's door in the same moment.*)

NEIL . . . to hell with this . . .
He is leaning forward towards the ignition key, but Pooley grabs his arm, pulling him up and out of the car. Neil resists, pulling back and— in doing so—strikes the side of his forehead on the doorframe. If possible, this slight scuffle should be shot in such a way that we are not clear what has happened. All we do know is that Neil is now out of the car and holding

12

his head, looking at his hand for any sign of blood:

NEIL Bloody marvellous, that is . . .

POOLEY Are you all right?

It's a perfunctory question. Neil hardly seems in danger of collapse.

NEIL Oh—yeah—sure—only got my flaming head bashed in . . .

POOLEY . . . let's have a look . . .

NEIL . . . just—pack it up, will you?

Pooley looks at him for a moment. Then makes to lean into the car and reach for the holdall. But Neil bars his way.

NEIL That's my bag. You'll leave it alone.

POOLEY All right, Mr Whatever-your-name-is. We'll sort this out at the station.

NEIL You're damned right we will.

The Station Office

Coombes coming through with a file. As he moves to his desk, Pooley comes through the main entrance with Neil who carries the holdall. Coombes simply glances at them, gets on with his work. There is nothing unusual about someone being brought in.

The Charge Room

The light comes on. Pooley comes in with Neil. Pooley moves to a chair by the table, swings it round, brusquely indicating for Neil to sit, and moves to the door to call.

POOLEY Harry!

Neil moves towards the table, puts the holdall on it. Sits. Takes off gloves and puts them on table. Lights a cigarette. Coombes enters.

POOLEY Sarge in?

COOMBES Just come back.

POOLEY Keep an eye on this one while I have a word with him, will you?

He goes out. Coombes remains. Looks at Neil who glares back angrily. Coombes crosses, opens a drawer, produces the ashtray, puts it before Neil. Neil—as though suddenly remembering—produces his handkerchief, dabs it against his forehead, examines it, unsuccessfully, for fresh bleeding.

COOMBES What's it all about then?

NEIL Your friend's been giving me the strong-arm stuff, that's what it's all about.

COOMBES (*a friendly smile*) Pooley? Can't believe that.

NEIL . . . what are you—the comic relief or something?

There is an awkward moment. And then, as though suddenly aware of an unnecessary insult to this much-older man.

NEIL Sorry.

COOMBES That's all right, son: used to be "blue-bottles"—now it's "pig".
The only thing that hasn't changed is the wages.
Neil dabs at his forehead again, glances at the handkerchief.

NEIL Pooley, did you say?

COOMBES That's right: Constable Pooley.

NEIL I'm gonna have your friend Pooley.
Close-up of Coombes. His face shows nothing.

NEIL You bloody see if I don't.
*He takes a pull at his cigarette. We hold the close-up of him a momen
before fading out.*

PART TWO
The Charge Room

*Coombes sits. Neil paces. Irritably, smoking, glancing at his watch.
Looks angrily at Coombes: gets no response.*

The Sergeant's Office

Pooley is with Ken, who sits feet up on the desk.

POOLEY I ask him what's in the bag and he tells me to get knotted: you
know . . . coming the Big "I am". Then he tries to start the car
so I grab him . . .

KEN . . . this was in Plough Street?

POOLEY Just round the corner from the jewellers'.

KEN You're sure he was on his own?

POOLEY I waited before I spoke to him: I didn't see anybody.

KEN But there could have been another one.

POOLEY Could have been.
The door opens and Smith puts his head in.

SMITH Nobody wanting me, is there?

KEN *(shakes head)* How d'you get on?

SMITH Waste of time.
He makes to leave, but Ken calls him.

KEN Smithy . . . are you off?

SMITH *(irritably)* What does that mean?

KEN *(equally irritable)* Look—are you off or aren't you?

SMITH Few notes to write up—why?

KEN Might have something for you on those break-ins.
*There is a pause. Smith shows little response, but just looks at Ken. Then
he is nodding briefly and goes out. Ken stands.*

KEN Right, let's have a word with him.

14

The Charge Room

Coombes and Neil who is now sitting and just stubbing out his cigarette end. The door opens and Ken comes in. Coombes stands. Neil almost follows suit, then thinks better of it. Ken will be pleasant. But underneath it we should sense the iron fist.

KEN Mr Yeldham?

NEIL Yes.

KEN Your full name please, Mr Yeldham.
He nods to Coombes who starts to jot down notes.

NEIL (*wearily*) Neil Edward Yeldham.

KEN How old are you, Mr Yeldham?

NEIL Twenty-three. (*Smiles flatly.*) 26th of March, 1950. Aries.

KEN Your address?

NEIL (*hesitates slightly before*) 84 Leicester Road, Northampton.

KEN Now I must ask you to turn out your pockets.

NEIL Why?

KEN Because you're under arrest, Mr Yeldham: let's not be difficult, eh?
After a moment's pause, Neil takes various items from his pockets and bangs them, one by one, down on the table. They include a small wallet and his keys. Neil watches, anger suppressed, as Ken takes up the wallet, takes out the driving licence, flips it open to verify the address he was given, returns the licence to wallet, wallet to table. Ken takes up the car keys.

KEN Borrow your car keys for a few minutes.

NEIL Why?

KEN Just like to have a look at your car, that's all: you'll get them back.
He moves to the door and goes out.

The Station Office

Pooley waits. Straightens up as Ken comes through and tosses the keys at him.

KEN Let's have that car checked out.

POOLEY Right, sarge.

KEN While you're there—check the lockups—especially that jewellers.
Pooley nods and goes out.

The Charge Room

Ken opens the door and jerks his head for Coombes to come outside.

The corridor

KEN *(as Coombes comes out, pulling the door shut)* Get on to records, will you, Harry—see if he's got form. *(Makes to move back.)* And you'd better check that address with Northampton.

The Charge Room

Ken comes in. He is still pleasant, but with that firm undertone.

KEN I understand from my constable that you refuse to open this bag.

NEIL That's right.

KEN And you still refuse?

NEIL *(slight pause)* Hardly any point, is there?

Ken unzips the bag and methodically takes out the contents to put them on the table . . . a shirt, tie, pullover, toilet bag, change of underwear. The toilet bag is opened and briefly inspected. Ken returns everything with equal method, does up the zip.

NEIL Do you mind telling me what you're looking for?

KEN Could be anything.

NEIL I see.

KEN Jewellery perhaps.

NEIL I occasionally wear cuff-links.

KEN Smart.

NEIL I want to see the senior officer.

KEN The man in charge, you mean?

NEIL That's what I mean.

KEN You're seeing him.

Neil's attitude will now change, albeit slightly, now that he knows he's dealing with the guvnor. Ken has taken up the gloves from the table, briefly looked at them, put them down.

NEIL You've no right to treat me like this . . .

KEN . . . you may not think so, Mr Yeldham—but we've got every right.

NEIL Then perhaps you'd tell me what I'm supposed to have done.

KEN Perhaps you'll tell me what you were doing there at this time of night.

NEIL That's my affair.

KEN That depends.

NEIL On what?

KEN On what we know and you say you don't.

Neil looks at him. Then gives a sort of laugh as though suddenly aware of the lunacy of the situation.

NEIL You're treating me like a criminal.

KEN If you're not, you've got nothing to worry about . . .

16

NEIL . . . nothing to . . . you pull me out of my own car . . . drag me to a police station in the middle of the night . . .

KEN . . . you chose the time, we didn't . . .

NEIL . . . bloody South Africa . . .

KEN . . . you were being questioned by a police officer. You refused to answer those questions. He asked you to get out of your car instead of which you tried to drive away . . .

NEIL . . . he said that?

KEN Didn't you?

NEIL . . . if he said I tried to drive away he's a liar . . .

KEN . . . what's your version?

NEIL (*"patiently"*) He told me to get out of the car. I realised there was no point in arguing with someone like him so I went to get out. Out of sheer . . . second nature . . . I went to take out the ignition key and the next thing I know is that I'm being hauled off my feet—and you think that's doing his duty.

KEN I know he was doing his duty.

NEIL Then God help us.

KEN During the past two months we've had five break-ins in this area: we've got reason to believe that a Cortina is being used. At half past twelve in the morning you're seen in the right sort of car in the right sort of area. You're questioned and you don't give any satisfactory answers. That's why my officer brought you in and that's why he was right.

NEIL Do I look like a bloody criminal?

   Ken looks at him for a moment. Then opens a filing cabinet, takes out a handful of photographs, tosses them onto the table.

KEN You pick out the criminal—I'll give you a medal.

   They look at each other.

The side street

The Panda car is parked near the Cortina. Pooley has all the Cortina doors open so that the interior light is on. He is searching the boot with his torch. He slams the boot down. His search clearly in vain. He stands a moment somewhat frustrated. Then he takes up his radio and calls through to the station.

The Charge Room

Coombes enters.

COOMBES Have a word, sarge?

The corridor

Ken and Coombes are outside the Charge Room door.

COOMBES   Pooley just called in: nothing on the car.

KEN   (*nods*) Shops?

COOMBES   Checking now.

Ken nods. Coombes jerks his head towards the Charge Room door.

COOMBES   Waddya reckon?

Ken clicks his teeth, gives a little jerk of the head. He is clearly unsure.

KEN   Let me know as soon as he gets back on.

The Charge Room

Neil scarcely looks up as Ken comes in.

KEN   You know . . . the whole thing would be a lot easier if you told us what you were doing there.

It was a bad move: Neil is intelligent enough to see it.

NEIL   I'll tell you what I told him: I was sitting in my car, minding my own business.

KEN   Now it's our business.

NEIL   Because you made it so: no other reason.

There is a slight pause.

KEN   All right, Mr Yeldham. Cards on the table. I'm not satisfied.

NEIL   . . . you're treating me like a criminal . . .

KEN   . . . you said . . .

NEIL   . . . is that all you can . . .

KEN   . . . "suspected person" . . .

NEIL   Words.

KEN   For the time being.

NEIL   Let me get one thing clear . . . I'm under arrest—right?

KEN   Arrested on suspicion—right.

NEIL   Right.

KEN   Been brought in before, have you?

NEIL   No I bloody haven't.

KEN   You sure?

NEIL   Look it up.

KEN   We are.

NEIL   (*It takes a moment to go home*) Do you mean you're checking up on me?

KEN   That's right. (*Neil's face shows exactly what he thinks of that.*) Start again then . . .

NEIL   . . . no, no—just a minute . . . you mean you're actually checking up to see if I've got a record?

KEN   . . . that's what I mean . . .

18

NEIL . . . Good God Almighty . . .

KEN . . . I said we'll start again: what are you doing in Broadstone at this time of night?

Now another slight shift in Neil's attitude. He will answer curtly, quickly . . . subconsciously perhaps driving on to the inevitable conclusion.

NEIL I live here.

KEN You said Northampton.

NEIL I stay with my girl-friend. You know: the permissive society.

KEN You were with her tonight then?

NEIL That's right.

KEN Name?

NEIL Ruth Forman.

KEN Address?

NEIL 24, Popham Terrace.

KEN What time did you leave her?

NEIL How romantic.

KEN Don't be smart.

NEIL Just before twelve.

KEN To go where?

NEIL Manchester.

KEN Why?

NEIL Business.

KEN What—three-hour drive? Manchester at three in the morning...

NEIL I'm like that.

KEN Throw you out, did she?

NEIL Mind your own damned business.

KEN So why didn't you drive to Manchester? (*Ken moves to the door and opens it to call:*) Harry! (*Looking at Neil.*) I'll give you another word: co-operation.

NEIL I'll give you one: victimisation.

Coombes comes in. Ken indicates for him to stay and goes out. Coombes moves in, sits, takes out a packet of cigarettes, takes one, on second thought offers one to Neil who refuses it with a look. Coombes lights his cigarette. A moment. Neil takes up his cigarettes, finds the packet empty, tosses it away. Coombes gets out his packet, holds it out to Neil. After hesitating, Neil takes a cigarette. Lights it for himself.

NEIL You got any family?

COOMBES A lad about your age.

NEIL Proud of his old man, is he?

COOMBES Brings his friends home, if that's what you mean.

Neil gives a derisive little jerk of the head. Then, suddenly remembers, dabs a finger against the slight wound on his forehead.

19

COOMBES How's the head?

NEIL (*giving a flat smile*) You do try.

The CID Office

Ken is with Smith, who sits hunched up, hands in the pockets of his topcoat.

KEN What d'you think—let him go?

SMITH You've been on to records.

KEN Waiting for 'em now.

SMITH Wait, then. (*There is a pause.*) Want me to . . . ?

KEN . . . I'll manage.

Smith grins at the result of his deliberate goad.

KEN (*uneasily*) I dunno, Smithy . . .

SMITH You told Pooley to keep his eyes open—right?

KEN . . . right . . .

SMITH . . . he's turned up a possibility—right . . . ?

KEN . . . right . . .

SMITH . . . what do you want—catch'em being on the job all the time? Where's the satisfaction in that? Want to make the likes of me redundant?

KEN (*irritated*) . . . you know what I'm talking about . . .

SMITH . . . you've got a suspect. You had one last year . . .

KEN . . . I've been waiting for that . . .

SMITH . . . you let him go because he was clever enough to brazen it out and he'd done twelve more jobs before we caught up with him again . . .

KEN . . . yeah, yeah . . .

SMITH . . . you're doing your job: people don't like it but they also don't like their shops being broken into. It's inconvenient, makes a mess . . . puts the insurance rates up . . . which means we all pay. Waddya want—an excuse? (*His flat smile.*) No problem.

The telephone rings.

SMITH 'Phone.

Ken looks at him, then he takes up the 'phone.

The Station Office

Pooley comes in and moves through to

The Charge Room

Neil and Coombes look up as Pooley comes in.

POOLEY Sarge?

COOMBES In with Smithy.

Pooley nods. There is a slight look between him and Neil. Pooley exits.

The CID Office

Ken is just replacing the receiver as there is a tap at the door and Pooley enters.

POOLEY *(to Smith)* Sorry, sarge. *(To Ken.)* All O.K?

KEN *(nods)* Northampton's just been on—they've checked his address—he lives in digs. Landlady says he stays out all night— once, maybe twice a week.

SMITH Interesting.

KEN *(slight shake of the head)* Says he stays with his girl-friend—with her tonight.

POOLEY Looks like he's in the clear then.

SMITH Not yet, son—not yet. *(He's on his feet . . . a sudden burst of vitality.)* Possibilities. One. He's on his own, waiting to do the job. No breaking gear found on him, so unlikely. Two. He's done the job. Nothing found on him, no signs of breaking, and he'd hardly be sitting there. Very unlikely. Three. He's working with someone else—remember, witness says he thought there were two men in the car. You come along, other one gets a smell, hops it Highly possible. Four. He just happens to be sitting there at half past twelve in the morning. *(The flat smile returns.)* You does your duty and you takes your choice.

POOLEY I had to pull him in, sarge.

KEN . . . you'd have been for the high jump if you hadn't . . .

POOLEY . . . he was just being—you know—bloody awkward . . .

KEN . . . yeah. Okay. Wait downstairs.

Pooley goes out.

SMITH With his girl friend, he says.

KEN Says.

SMITH Worth a visit.

KEN I'll send Pooley.

SMITH No, no—I'll go.

KEN Ten minutes ago you were dead beat.

SMITH I wake up about this time of the morning. I've got a theory about it.

KEN Hazard of the profession.

SMITH Job. *(Holds out hand.)* Address?

The Station Office

Pooley leans on the counter, writing up his notebook. Smith moves past him and goes out. A moment later, Ken comes through. Pooley doesn't see

21

him and for a moment Ken stands looking at Pooley . . . there's a slight trace of doubt: he knows what an arrogant bastard Pooley can be.

KEN Take over from Harry, will you?

Pooley nods, takes up his notebook and moves away.

The Charge Room

Pooley comes in. He indicates that Coombes should leave. He does so. Then Pooley sits. Neil looks at him with a mixture of distaste and scorn. Then Pooley takes up his notebook, checks his notes. The camera holds them a moment; these two young men of similar age but totally different persuasions.

Ruth's sitting room

Ruth is coming through from the bedroom, in nightie, pulling on a house-coat. As she moves, there is a discreet tapping at the door. She believes the caller to be Neil: her attitude is complacent rather than concerned. She doesn't bother to button the housecoat. She moves through— without turning on the light.

Her small hallway

Ruth comes through from the sitting room and opens the door to Smith. Immediately, her attitude changes to one of surprise and concern. She closes the door as much as possible.

SMITH Miss Forman?

RUTH What do you want?

Smith holds out his warrant card: he'd had it ready.

SMITH Detective-Sergeant Smith: if I could have a word?

RUTH *(She is staring, without really seeing, at the warrant.)* You woke me up . . .

SMITH I'm sorry . . .

RUTH What time is it . . . ?

SMITH I won't keep you long . . .

RUTH What is it . . . ?

SMITH You know a Mr Yeldham . . .

RUTH Oh my God . . . what's happened . . . ?

SMITH If I could just come inside . . .

After a moment, she steps aside and lets him in.

RUTH He's been in an accident, hasn't he? I knew it . . .

SMITH . . . nothing like that, Miss Forman. *(Indicates.)* Through here? *She leads him into the sitting room. Turns on the light. Realises her housecoat is undone, fastens it. Smith is looking round the room. His eyes return to her. He gives his smile.*

22

SMITH We're making some enquiries—Mr Yeldham might be able to help us.

RUTH Neil?

SMITH If you could just verify . . .

RUTH . . . do you mean he's in trouble with the police?

SMITH . . . we don't know. Trouble, I mean. (*Smiles.*) Which is why I'm here.

She sits, almost lights a cigarette, thinks better of it, still quite numbed at what's happened.

SMITH He was with you tonight. (*She nods.*) What time did he leave?

RUTH About half past eleven, perhaps a little later—why?

SMITH Where was he going?

RUTH To Manchester.

SMITH Straight there?

RUTH As far as I know.

SMITH He didn't though, did he?

RUTH How would I know?

SMITH No. Of course you wouldn't. Known him long?

RUTH Three months or so—why?

SMITH Stay here often, does he?

RUTH Once or twice a week, perhaps. (*Smith nods.*) It's not a crime.

SMITH None of my business.

RUTH Then why ask?

SMITH Morals—no. Facts—yes.

RUTH God: you really are what people say you are . . .

SMITH Me?

RUTH Police.

SMITH (*smiles*) That.

RUTH You come bursting in here . . .

SMITH . . . bursting?

RUTH . . . drag me out of bed . . .

SMITH . . . I said I'm sorry . . .

RUTH . . . not even saying why.

SMITH . . . one way of finding out.

RUTH . . . finding out what?

SMITH . . . if you know why. People do. All sorts of people. The most unlikely sorts of people. You'd be surprised.

RUTH Not any more.

He looks at her. He moves away. He sees a new-looking transistor radio.

SMITH (*pointing to the radio*) Nice.

RUTH Would you like to see the receipt?

SMITH (*He looks. The smile.*) Here's my problem, Miss Forman—see if

23

you can help. What would your Mr Yeldham be doing, sitting in a car, down a side street, half-past twelve in the morning—one hour after he left you and on his way to Manchester.

RUTH I've no idea.

SMITH Neither have we. And your Mr Yeldham isn't making it easy for us.

RUTH Is it really that important?

SMITH (*Her tone says it all. Smith looks at her for a moment.*) You a student?

RUTH Yes.

SMITH My daughter's a student. Posters on the wall: the occasional demo. She wouldn't think it was important either. But it could be. Not to you, not to her. But. (*And now with an increasing edge.*) Which is why I burst into your house, drag you up, ask a lot of damn-fool silly questions. Between you and me, Miss Forman, I'd much rather be at home putting my big cold copper's feet into my nice, warm, marital bed. Now, I don't know much about dropping bombs in Vietnam . . . but what I do know is that as long as shops get broken into, old ladies get damaged for a shilling, kids get lured into cars and assaulted . . . as long as what is loosely termed "the human race" fouls up the pavements instead of making daisy-chains, there'll always be nasty little, power-happy little establishment lackeys like me asking a lot of law-abiding citizens like you stupid questions like this. I don't want to be here, Miss Forman . . . I have—as they say—a job to do. Now. When I came through that door you said . . . "What's happened . . . he's been in an accident . . . I knew it". Knew what, Miss Forman?

RUTH (*after a pause*) It was the—mood he was in. We'd had a row. That's why he—left—at that time.

SMITH Sulky sort of chap, is he?

RUTH (*almost objects, but*) Difficult. (*Smiles to herself.*) He'd prefer that.

SMITH So the chances are . . . he was sitting in that car . . . feeling sorry for himself . . . wondering whether or not to come back here . . . right?

RUTH It happens.

SMITH It's happened to me, Miss Forman. Why the bloody hell couldn't he say so? Don't bother to answer—just tell me where your 'phone is and then we can all get to bed.

The Station Office

The telephone is ringing. Ken comes through and takes it up.

KEN Broadstone Police, Sergeant Ridgeway. Smithy. Yeah, they've

24

just been through. Nothing known. Yeah. Yeah. I'll send him on his way then. Cheers.

Ruth's hallway

Smith is replacing telephone receiver. He moves into Ruth's sitting room.

Ruth's sitting room

SMITH Thanks.

RUTH (*stiffly*) Don't mention it.
She gets up, moves to him.

Ruth's hallway

She opens the main door. He almost goes, but turns to speak.

SMITH I—er—I didn't mean to sound off like that.

RUTH (*she smiles*) I hope you don't wake your wife up, that's all.

SMITH (*smiles*) Blue murder. If I hadn't come round here, it would have meant keeping him 'til morning.

RUTH You've just thought of that.

SMITH Could be.

RUTH If I were you, I'd be very nice to him from now on: if there's one think he can't stand, it's people shoving him around.

The Charge Room

Ken comes in. He nods for Pooley to exit. Pooley does.

KEN Sorry to have kept you, Mr Yeldham. I'm sure you appreciate why we had to do it.

NEIL You mean I can go.

KEN That's right.

NEIL Just like that.

KEN Not very pleasant, I know it wasn't . . .

NEIL . . . I want an apology.
There is a slight pause. This is what Ken has been half-expecting.

KEN I apologise for the inconvenience certainly . . .

NEIL That isn't what I mean. I want an apology on the grounds that I should never have been brought here in the first place.

KEN I've already explained, Mr Yeldham. The constable was doing his duty . . .

NEIL . . . not from where I stand.

The Station Office

Pooley is waiting. Ken comes through. He doesn't look at Pooley, but calls.

KEN Harry! (*Coombes comes through.*) Take a statement form through

to Mr Yeldham, will you? (*Coombes looks at him, glances a Pooley.*) Doesn't trust me—wants to make it out himself.
Coombes collects up a statement form and exits. Already the suspicion is in Pooley's mind, but he tries to make light of it.

POOLEY What's this then, sarge?

KEN (*stiffly*) He wants to make a statement while it's still clear in his mind—all right?

POOLEY While what's clear?

KEN He's making a complaint, Pooley: unlawful arrest and assault. That's what he wants to get clear.
Close up of Pooley and then fade out.

PART THREE
The Charge Room

Neil is writing, obviously remembering. The door opens, Coombes comes in with a cup of tea. He puts it down without comment, makes to go out. He's almost at the door, when:

NEIL Thanks.
Coombes goes out. Neil looks at the tea, gives a sardonic little jerk of the head, and goes back to his writing.

The Sergeant's Office

Pooley is worried but stubborn in his belief. Ken remains calm, quiet, insistent.

KEN You asked him to get out of the car.

POOLEY (*puffs out cheeks*) I asked him what was in the bag, he told me to mind my own business, so I asked him to get out of the car.

KEN I'd change your tone if I were you, Pooley—your future might depend on it.

POOLEY I mean—bloody hell, sarge—what was I supposed to do?

KEN I'm not asking what you were supposed to do—I'm asking what you did. Right. You asked him to get out . . .

POOLEY I asked him to get out and he makes to start the engine . . .

KEN He says he was taking the key out.

POOLEY Then he's a liar.

KEN He'll say the same thing.

POOLEY As far as I knew, he was going to start the engine and hop it. I couldn't just stand there . . .

KEN . . . so you grabbed him . . .

POOLEY . . . when I saw him going for the keys . . .

KEN . . . yeah, yeah . . . all right. (*Slight pause.*) You went to get him out of the car and he banged his head.

POOLEY I wouldn't have pulled him if he hadn't resisted. I asked him to get out, he wouldn't. As for his head . . . he hardly touched it . . . and not even that if he hadn't decided to make a fight of it.

KEN But you saw his head was cut.

POOLEY I saw him holding it, so I asked him if he was all right. He starts ranting and raving about his head being bashed in—you know the way some of 'em carry on. You've only got to get within spitting distance and they're hollering blue murder. I mean, bloody hell, sarge . . . what was I supposed to do? I didn't go charging in there, waving me stick . . . I asked him all the questions, gave him every chance to be reasonable, but he just wasn't having any. He'd made up his mind from the word go: you could see it. One of these smart-arses who knows his rights: you know the sort . . . looking down their noses . . . calling you "officer" . . . trying to make you look small . . .

KEN (who has listened to this with a growing suspicion)
. . . what are you getting so worked up about . . . ?

POOLEY . . . not worked-up, sarge . . . you know . . .

KEN . . . this thing goes through, you start puffing and blinding like that and you'll have trouble.

POOLEY (quietly) Sarge.

The Station Office

Coombes is working. Smith comes in through the main doors.

SMITH Where's Ken—in his office?

COOMBES I wouldn't go in for a minute if I were you, Smithy. (*Smith looks at him.*) He's got problems.

The Sergeant's Office

Ken is trying to get at the truth. He still doesn't raise his voice, has no need to.

KEN You didn't lose your temper? (*Pooley hesitates.*) Well?

POOLEY You know, sarge . . .

KEN No I don't bloody know . . . which is why I'm asking.

POOLEY He was deliberately having a go . . .

KEN . . . I'm not asking about him, I'm asking about you.

POOLEY . . . I might have got a bit shirty . . .

KEN . . . that why they pay you, is it? To get shirty? To get clever?

POOLEY What was I supposed to do? Get on me hands and knees? Offer him a bunch of flowers?

KEN Don't get smart with me, Pooley . . .

POOLEY . . . for Christ's sake, sarge . . . he could have pulled anything . . . you know the way some of 'em try and bluff it out . . .

KEN . . . did you or did you not provoke him?

POOLEY . . . I did what I thought was right. I did what I'm supposed to do. He was looking for trouble from the word go . . .

KEN . . . so you keep saying.

POOLEY Well it's true.

KEN It wasn't his attitude you pulled him in for though, was it? Was it, Pooley?

POOLEY (*after a slight pause*) It's just that . . . sometimes I . . . (*He trails off.*)

KEN Sometimes you what?

POOLEY It doesn't matter . . .

KEN . . . sometimes you what?

POOLEY . . . sometimes I've had enough, that's all.

KEN You what? Ten minutes in the force and you've had enough? You should have been a bloody ballet dancer . . .

POOLEY . . . I didn't mean that . . .

KEN . . . well what did you mean?

POOLEY I meant tonight.

KEN Something special about tonight, is there?

POOLEY It doesn't matter, sarge . . .

KEN . . . come on, Pooley—what's so special about tonight?

POOLEY I'm not a machine. Not something you switch on and off. I'm entitled to get fed up at times . . .

KEN . . . about what?

POOLEY About the way people go on. On and on and on. Why are you a copper? What are your qualifications? How much dropsy do you take . . .

KEN . . . is that what he said?

POOLEY . . . not him. (*Ken waits, forcing him to go on.*) I went round to my girl's tonight. There was this—fellah. Showing off. You know—trying to put me down.

KEN And that stuck in your throat, did it?

POOLEY (*Pooley tries to make light of it with a little shrug.*) Maybe I need a tonic or something.

KEN (*slowly and carefully*) So when you met our friend in there, you were in a bit of a mood.

POOLEY He fitted the description of the bloke we were looking for. That's why I spoke to him, that's why I brought him in.

KEN You're quite sure you didn't go out tonight . . . looking for trouble.

POOLEY That's what you think, is it, sarge?

KEN Wait in the office: I might want you.
Pooley leaves.

The Station Office

Coombes is working. He glances up at Pooley coming through. Pooley sits on the visitor's seat. A moment. Pooley looks up. Coombes is working. Pooley takes up his cap and nervously revolves it in his hands.

The Sergeant's Office

On Ken a moment. Then Smith comes in and sits in "his" chair.

SMITH (*Ken gives a little jerk of the head.*) Writing up his notes, is he?

KEN His privilege.

SMITH Nothing I can do, is there?

KEN Such as?

SMITH (*Smith "smiles" and stands.*) I'm for bed, then. (*Ken nods. Smith moves to the door, but:*) Oh yeah . . . his girl friend says to tell him if he's got any sense he'll spend the rest of the night at her place.

KEN Pity he didn't stay there earlier.

SMITH They had a row.

KEN A what?

SMITH That's what he was doing there. In the car. Sulking. He's like that. Or so she reckons. See you in the morning. (*He's about to go, but:*)

KEN Hang on a bit, Smithy . . . tell me more.

The Charge Room

Neil is writing. He stops. He has a sudden moment of doubt. But then he presses on.

The Station Office

Pooley is sitting. He glances up as Smith moves past with:

SMITH (*genially*) See you tomorrow.
Coombes mumbles "Goodnight, Smithy". Pooley doesn't feel up to pleasantries. Ken comes through. Pooley stands. Ken moves directly to him, speaks soft, fast, direct.

KEN You pulled him out of that car because you thought he was going to make off—and for no other reason.

POOLEY That's the truth, sarge.
Ken nods and moves quickly away. Pooley sits.

The Charge Room

Neil writing. A moment. Ken comes in. He is holding a small booklet, actually a copy of the Criminal Law Act 1967. Neil looks at him. Hold this a moment.

NEIL Nearly finished.

KEN Take your time.

NEIL Someone else moving in, is there?

KEN Not that sort of night.
A moment.

NEIL I suppose you think I'm just being damned awkward. (*Ken gives a somewhat non-committal little jerk of the head.*) I can assure you I'm not doing this just for the fun of it . . .

KEN . . . you think you've got a grievance—that's fair enough.

NEIL . . . what's happened to me tonight isn't important . . .

KEN . . . it's the principle.

NEIL . . . you think that's funny.

KEN . . . I think you'd like to think I do . . .

NEIL . . . so you can chalk me up as just another trouble-maker . . .

KEN . . . I'm not chalking you up as anything . . .

NEIL Don't be too complacent, sergeant: you've chosen the wrong man. *There is a slight pause. Frankly, Ken would like to kick him up the arse. But:*

KEN Which particular "principle" are we talking about?

NEIL It's called "the freedom of the individual".

KEN Tricky word that—"freedom".

NEIL . . . then let me give you my version: one of your constables has behaved in a way that completely exceeds his duty—without reason—and worse, without any form of redress from a superior officer—you, sergeant. What happened to me tonight was interference for the sake of interference and you know it. It happens all the time.

KEN Does it?

NEIL Read your newspapers.

KEN I'll tell you what I have read, Mr Yeldham: this . . . (*He tips the booklet onto the table.*) The Criminal Law Act, 1967. I think you ought to read it. Section 2, sub-sections 4 and 5.

NEIL I'd rather you just told me . . .

KEN . . . roughly speaking, it says this, Mr Yeldham: a constable may arrest, without warrant, any person whom he—with reasonable cause—suspects either to be guilty of an offence or about to commit an offence. (*Slight pause.*) Reasonable suspicion, Mr Yeldham.

NEIL I'd say that's just about the biggest attack on civil liberty that's ever been set on paper . . .

KEN . . . Section 2, sub-sections 4 and 5.

NEIL Don't people like you ever stop to think what this means? Anyone . . . at any time, can be stopped and pulled in—just when you feel like it

KEN . . . the duty of a police constable is clearly defined in this Act . . . my constable was doing his duty according to the book . . .

NEIL . . . like hell he was.

KEN . . . but then, you're not just concerned with what happened to you: it's the principle. It's not just the individual constable you're complaining about, is it? It's the system which gives him his authority . . .

NEIL . . . give the police this sort of power and God knows what use they'll put it to . . .

KEN . . . "reasonable suspicion" . . .

NEIL You think that's protection enough?

KEN I think it just about balances out.

NEIL Then what "reasonable suspicion" did he have?

KEN Enough to satisfy me, Mr Yeldham.

NEIL I'd hardly expect anything else.

KEN Closing the ranks, is it?

NEIL Isn't it?

KEN He was told to keep a lookout for a car which we have reason to believe was being used in a series of break-ins. A car like yours, Mr Yeldham . . . a dark blue Cortina with a "J" registration . . .

NEIL . . . my car is grey . . .

KEN . . . at night-time the witness could have been mistaken . . .

NEIL (*of his notes*) I'll put it down anyway . . .

KEN . . . you were seen at half past twelve in the morning . . .

NEIL . . . you make it sound like the middle of the night . . .

KEN . . . town this size? Gone half past midnight on a Sunday? We're not talking about the big city, we're talking about here. In a side street, near the back entrance to a jewellers . . . he asks what you're doing there . . . you won't tell him . . . he asks what's in the bag you're carrying . . . you won't tell him that, either. And you still say he wasn't carrying out his duty?

NEIL Exceeding his duty . . .

KEN According to you, Mr Yeldham—but not according to the book. (*He raps knuckles against the booklet on the table.*) Suppose it was your car . . . it had been stolen . . . suppose it was your shop . . . it

31

had been broken into . . . suppose you found out he'd seen someone sitting in the car and just strolled on by—what about his duty then? Or suppose you were a hard-case—sitting there with a shotgun ready to blow his face off? Because that happens, Mr Yeldham—like you say, it's all in the papers—there's one or two coppers' widows who'll put you very straight about that one.

NEIL I'm well aware that the police have a job to do . . .

KEN I sometimes wonder . . .

NEIL What I'm talking about is the man's attitude . . .

KEN Overbearing, was he? Pompous? Typical copper? There you are, sitting in your car, minding your own business, and up he comes, sticking his nose in. D'you know what, Mr Yeldham? I would have felt as irritated as you did . . . because you were irritated, weren't you, Mr Yeldham?

NEIL Obviously . . .

KEN . . . what did you say when he first spoke to you?

NEIL I can't remember . . .

KEN . . . he can. Put it down in your statement. "I'm thinking." That's what you said.

NEIL Probably.

KEN "I'm thinking. Some of us do it, y'know." Why did you say that, I wonder, Mr Yeldham?

NEIL . . . it was one of those stupid things you say . . .

KEN . . . think about it. "Some of us." Implication, would you call it? Or a downright bloody insult? Say that to the wrong sort of fellah in a pub and you might get a glass down your throat. And before you start thinking I'm making excuses for him—you're wrong. What I'm saying is that what you call his "attitude" was inevitable when someone gives the sort of answers you gave. You're an educated man: think about it. (*Neil gives a cynical little jerk of the head.*) You refused to open that holdall for him—why? There was nothing in it . . .

NEIL . . . precisely . . .

KEN . . . you opened it for me . . .

NEIL . . . as I said at the time—there was hardly any point . . .

KEN . . . then what was the point before? Who was being awkward then? And don't tell me you know your rights, Mr Yeldham—because according to this—(*Of the booklet.*)—you don't.

NEIL You seem to forget that I was dragged out of my car . . .

KEN . . . did he ask you to get out?

NEIL . . . I shouldn't think he knows the meaning of the word . . .

32

KEN . . . you mean without any warning, he opens the car door . . .

NEIL . . . I mean he told me to get out.

KEN . . . how many times—once—twice?

NEIL . . . probably . . .

KEN . . . and you still refused . . .

NEIL . . . I was getting out of the car when he started pulling at me . . .

KEN . . . without any reason—he jerks open the car door and grabs you?

NEIL . . . no reason whatsoever . . .

KEN . . . what if you were reaching for the key—trying to start the engine . . .

NEIL . . . I was taking the key out.

KEN But you could have been turning on the engine.
He is leaning over the table as he talks. Suddenly raises his arm. Instinctively Neil puts up a protective arm.

KEN I could have been taking a swipe at you. You had about half a second to make up your mind.

NEIL (*slight pause*) I'd say that was a pretty cheap way of failing to make a point.

KEN Both of you could have been mistaken, Mr Yeldham. That's all I'm asking you to consider.

NEIL You seem to be forgetting this.
He indicates the cut on his forehead.

KEN No, I'm not forgetting it.

NEIL "Reasonable suspicion" allows for this too, does it?

KEN You were resisting arrest . . .

NEIL . . . oh come on . . .

KEN What would you call it?

NEIL I was being dragged out of my car . . .

KEN You banged your head, he banged it . . . deliberate . . . accident . . . can you honestly say what happened? Would it ever have happened if you'd got out of the car when he asked you to? He believed one thing, you believed another . . . wasn't what happened inevitable . . . unfortunate maybe . . . unnecessary maybe . . . but inevitable?

NEIL It happened: that's all that matters.

KEN When you're ready I'll get someone to drive you back.
He moves to the door, but Neil stops him.

NEIL I'm sorry you couldn't persuade me to change my mind.

KEN Let me tell you the form, Mr Yeldham. Your complaint will be investigated by a Senior Police Officer—more than likely from another Force. He interviews Constable Pooley and takes

33

statements from everyone concerned. Your girl friend, for instance. She might be able to say what sort of mood you were in. Things like that. Because it's a criminal offence, the papers'll be sent to the Director of Public Prosecutions. He'll decide whether to institute proceedings against the constable or whether there's not enough evidence to form the basis of a charge. You'll be informed in writing of his decision. If he decides there isn't enough evidence, you'll also be told that you're at liberty to institute your own proceedings—that is, of course, if you're not satisfied. Now a lot of people don't like the idea of police investigating police—and you, Mr Yeldham, being a man of principle—will no doubt agree with them. So if they go against you—you stick to your guns and go for a civil action . . . you never know your luck . . . get him into court and it might mean prison. (*Points at the desk.*) Make your statement, Mr Yeldham . . . you make quite sure you know your rights and you make your statement. I won't like it because whatever happens, it's a mark against me . . . but what I like even less is the thought of you walking around thinking you've been hard-done-by. So do it, Mr Yeldham. Make your statement, go home, and do it.

After looking at Neil for a moment, he turns and goes out.

The Station Office

Coombes is working. Pooley is waiting. Neil comes through. He carries his holdall. Coombes looks up.

NEIL The—er—the sergeant said something about a car.

COOMBES Waiting for you outside.

There is an awkward moment. Then Neil nods.

NEIL Goodnight.

COOMBES Cheers.

Neil moves to the main doors. Stops. Turns. Looks at Pooley. For a moment it looks as though Neil might say something. But he changes his mind and goes out.

The Sergeant's Office

KEN (*Ken is using the telephone.*) I'll get someone over first thing in the morning. Shaken up, was she? Yeah—no point tonight. Yeah. Cheers.

During this, Pooley has entered. Ken makes some notes.

POOLEY Waddya reckon then, sarge?

KEN (*still writing*) What do I think, Pooley? I think they'll find he

34

hasn't got a case. I think they'll send him a nice letter—and that'll be that. Unless he decides to take it further himself—if he can find a solicitor who thinks he's got a good enough case.

POOLEY Cocky bastard.

He moves to the door, but Ken looks up for the first time.

KEN Feeling pleased with yourself, are you, Pooley? Feeling good? Go on—get out.

Pooley goes

A street

A Panda car moving through the deserted night streets.

Pooley is driving. Thinking about what has gone before. The Panda pulls up near a small row of shops. Pooley gets out, checks the doorlocks. Moves to a recessed shop door. Sees the crumpled heap of a man lying in the doorway. Pooley looks at him, bends, lifts the man. It is the old man of earlier in the evening. Intercut between him and Pooley. The old man stirs. Pooley grimaces: the stink of booze. He renews his efforts to lift the man. As he does, an empty bottle falls from the old man's fingers. Pooley gets the man onto his feet. Suddenly the man lashes out and catches Pooley a round-handed blow on the side of the face. Intercut between Pooley and the old man who suddenly realises what he has done.

POOLEY Come on, grand-dad—let's get you home . . .

Pooley supports the old man towards the car. He helps him in, then gets behind the wheel to drive away.

FADE OUT

The End

A Right Dream of Delight
by Michael O'Neill and Jeremy Seabrook

The Cast
At Fontaine's US Headquarters:
The Chairman of Fontaine
The Company Secretary
Sociologist
Economist
At Fontaine's British Branch:
Robert Walsh, *a senior Director*
Madeleine, *his wife*
Personnel Manager
An announcer
A production Monitor
Doris Muddiman, *an employee*
Gerry, *her husband*
Paul, *their eighteen-year-old son*
Rose, *a friend of Doris*
Bill, *her husband,*
    both of whom also work at Fontaine
Ian, *another worker*
First Worker
Second Worker
Third Worker
Fourth Worker

A Right Dream of Delight

A large boardroom in Seattle, USA

The boardroom of Fontaine (incorporating the Pacific Coast Perfume and Toilet Water Company), seventeenth floor of the Everest Insurance Company building in Seattle, summer 1958.

On a large oval table, stands a paperweight: a brick, set in onyx and silver, and inscribed:

"A brick from the front porch of the original home of Mrs H. Weissmuller, Mother of Fontaine."

Around the table are eight thrones of padded buttoned leather, and large objets d'art are placed at visually strategic points in the room. On the table a profusion of maps, reports, graphs, analyses, market surveys, investment forecasts, etc.

Three executives of the firm, chairman, vice-chairman and company secretary, are in consultation with three experts—a market economist, a sociologist and an investment consultant.

They are deciding on a site for the overseas expansion of Fontaine, a production and distribution centre for Europe. Evidence of long hours of discussion drawing to a close.

ECONOMIST   . . . all the surplus labour in Federal Germany has been completely mopped up by the Wirtschaftswunder.

CHAIRMAN   The what?

ECONOMIST   The miracle. The economic miracle. And anyway labour costs there are skyrocketing.

CHAIRMAN   *(evidently turning to his own earlier idea)* I still say we liked France. I thought why not take Fontaine Cosmetics right to the heart of the perfume capital of the world itself?
(There is general consternation.)

SOCIOLOGIST   No. No. Impossible. French perfume connotes the ABs and the luxury market, and the luxury market is not Fontaine territory. France is a real non-starter.

CHAIRMAN   My daughter went to Grenoble last semester. She just loved it there.

SOCIOLOGIST   The evidence is overwhelmingly against France.

CHAIRMAN   *(ruminative)* Pity.

ECONOMIST   That leaves the UK.

CHAIRMAN   I was in the UK after the war. You had to eat and drink to a timetable. The bars close at nine-thirty, and you have to put a coin in a slot meter to get some heat.

SOCIOLOGIST   I think you'll find things have changed a great deal. The UK has the advantage over almost every other European country.

CHAIRMAN   You have a high cost of labour though.

SOCIOLOGIST   Ah—not necessarily. If we choose carefully we can find an area with no tradition of organised labour, and with attractively low wage levels.

ECONOMIST   The really appealing thing about UK is, its basic industries are in decline, and are throwing up a big potential new labour market. There are cities all over UK, any one of which would be perfect. Only two hours away from London. Communications are easy, and bulk transference costs are cheap. Yeah, as we see it, the advantages of the UK are, first, the availability of plant, and second, it's the doorway to Europe, and to the British Commonwealth—which includes, you remember, several African countries. . . .

SOCIOLOGIST   And darker skins lend themselves to a whole new range of products. And two thirds of the world, gentlemen, are in the darker pigmentation range.

CHAIRMAN   They don't even have drug stores in the UK. But of course— (*Becoming more enthusiastic.*) our network of lady distribution agents could release us from the stranglehold of established retailers. . . . (*Lyrical.*) We'll recruit nationwide. Every block, every community will have its Fontaine agent. Her home will be a beauty parlour, and she will spread beauty among her neighbours and girl-friends on a regular commission basis.

ECONOMIST   The UK has virtually no experience of direct selling. You could expect profit level to exceed forty per cent on each and every article sold.

(*There is an impressed silence.*)

CHAIRMAN   Yeh, UK sure has a lot to recommend it. . . . (*Reflective.*) And it's kind of green and friendly. . . . I think UK deserves Fontaine. Do you have a list of likely manufacturing places?

SOCIOLOGIST   Yes. (*Fumbles among papers. Reads.*) Hundred-mile radius from London—there's Wolverhampton, Leicester, Norwich, Ipswich, Nottingham, Birmingham, Coventry, Litchborough, Reading, Portsmouth . . . all have a thousand population or more.

CHAIRMAN   Litchborough, did you say Litchborough? I love Litchborough. Litchborough, I was there in 1946. I was at the Lower Netherford base there in Oxfordshire County. I like Litchborough.

Anybody not like Litchborough? (*Pause.*) We all like Litchborough. (*On the intercom.*) Get me two reservations direct Seattle
to Litchborough, UK, some time tomorrow.

SOCIOLOGIST Litchborough doesn't have an airport.

CHAIRMAN Oh. Well it soon will have.

The Muddimans' bathroom in Litchborough, England

*This is a prosperous working-class household: a bay-windowed terraced
street of substantial Edwardian villas.*

*The bathroom is rather cramped, and crowded with shelves, containing
Fontaine products: Fontaine Body-Dew, Fontaine Bath-Balme, Fontaine
Sea Dog after shave, Fontaine Blush 'n' Hush, Tiger Lily cologne,
Fontaine Fandango lotion, Moondust talc, Fontaine Memphis Rose
soap, etc.*

*Doris is seen in her slip. She stands in front of the wash basin, with an
aerosol deodorant spray in one hand, raising her arm. She applies a fore-
finger to the cap of the spray. A dying splutter of empty air from the can.*

*Doris shakes it, and directs the spray at her other armpit, empty. Gesture
of annoyance, she flings it into a pedal-operated disposal bin.*

DORIS Damn and blast the thing. (*She shouts downstairs.*) Gerry . . .
Gerry . . . the damn Body Dew's packed up on me. Get a new 'un
will you, there's twelve in a box at the top of the cellar. (*She
applies vitaminised Fontaine Skin Food to her face. She sits in front of the
glass, tight-lipped. Stream of thought as she puts on the cream and makes
up her face.*) I shall have to get him to drop me off at the Cake
Box. You can't go to work empty-handed on your birthday . . . I
wish I'd never mentioned me damn birthday . . . twenty-four
cakes at tenpence a time, that's um, hour and a half's overtime
gone down their greedy throats . . . still, you ain't old at forty-
three, not these days. . . . (*Surveying herself and stroking her neck.*) I
reckon I could take sommat with a jabot. I ain't gone scraggy . . .
Enter Paul, Doris's son. He is eighteen.

PAUL Dad says where've you hidden his glasses. (*He gives her the deodorant spray.*)

DORIS They're where he left them, wet through, on the wash basin.
(*Paul goes out. She deodorises herself.*) He never said nothing. He's
forgot me birthday as well. They're a damn good pair . . . still, it
could be worse, I could be working in face powder. I'd have to
buy eighty odd cakes then . . . you can't get to know each other
if there's eighty of you. Twenty-four's just right. They're friendly
but you don't get too thick with them. (*Rubbing her face with the tips
of her fingers.*) Lovely texture, don't clog your pores a bit. (*Putting

41

her dress on.) I wonder if he has remembered me birthday . . . a nice bunch of red roses, that's what I'd like . . . in a basket, with a round wicker handle . . . we're at a big disadvantage in this house. It's all right giving other people Fontaine gifts, but it's one thing that won't wash here . . .

Their kitchen

Breakfast is being cooked.

DORIS (*entering*) Pooh, smell of frying fat, sticks to your clothes all day long . . . cooked breakfasts on a Friday, I should think you've gone off your head.

GERRY Might get a wife one day, do it for me.

DORIS It'll have to be your next one then. I've got other things to do of a morning.

GERRY I ain't going to starve meself just cause you do. You rush and rip about till you ain't nothing but a bag of bones. You want to sit down and get some of this down you.

DORIS Oo I couldn't. (*Pats her chest.*) It gives me the acidity. You can give some to Paul though. It's that age you need it. We don't want him fainting over his Bunsen burners or whatever they are . . . but don't take all day over it. I want you to drop me off.

GERRY Drop y'off? Ain't you goin' in 's morning?

DORIS I've got to nip in the Cake Box. I want two dozen of sommat fancy for the girls on the pipettes.

GERRY You treating 'em? You was calling 'em everything under the sun last week, you hadn't got a good word for any of 'em. If you feel like giving anybody a treat, it ought to be me.

DORIS Yes I should like. Last treat I gev you, you fell asleep on me. Get on with your breakfast. The smell of it's making me sick. . . . I ain't seen Madge about for a day or two. I hope nothing's happened to her.

PAUL They took her away. Yesterday afternoon. The ambulance came for her. There was a great mob of women all round the front door. About half past two. They took her away on a stretcher.

DORIS There. I knew I hadn't seen her. (*Suddenly acrimonious.*) What was you doing in the street at half past two yesterday afternoon? Why wasn't you at school?

PAUL Games day. I can work better at home. They can't check up on you, it's all right.

DORIS Oo my God. Don't say you've started playing the wag from school, not at your age. You ought to set an example, being a prefect . . . you're putting your whole future at risk. There's more to it than just getting your A levels. There's hundred out to grab that scholarship; it's a hundred and fifty pounds a year down the drain if you throw that out the window. Rose has got her eye on it for her Keith.

PAUL I always come home early on games day. Anyway, her Keith's about as thick as she is. He's been in the sixth form three years, one O level a year—it's an annual event.

DORIS It only needs one person to see you walking down that road . . . these things get reported back to your Headmaster. Them scholarships depend on Fontaine (*Quoting.*) "being satisfied with the Headmaster's character assessment as well as academic attainment . . . " I've got it in black and white upstairs in my drawer . . . you let that slip through your fingers after all we've done and I'll never forgive you.

GERRY If he's fit to go to university, he'll get there on his own merits. He don't need Fontaine to push him. It's like all Fontaine's free offers, you'll find there's a catch in it somewhere. If you read the small print, you'd see he'll be tied to them three years after he's finished college at slave labour rates. Women. Can't see further than next week.

DORIS Oo, you can't bear to see nobody get on, can you? They can walk into top management at Fontaine with a degree behind them. They cross the Atlantic two or three times a week, and think no more about it . . . if you had you way, he'd be in somebody's back yard, cutting shoeleather for the rest of his life.

GERRY I've cut shoeleather, and I wouldn't wish it on me worst enemy. You're the one who wants to keep him back, by selling him to Fontaine. I hope to Christ he sets his sights a bit further than that after all we've done for him.

PAUL (*animated*) I've had that rotten scholarship rammed down me throat for as long as I can remember. I'm going to leave school now. Go abroad for a year or two, get some experience.

GERRY You can just see him doing it, can't you? He'd spend one night under canvas and come back here at half past one in the morning 'cause he'd got his feet wet. Be a damned good thing if he would. Learn to support himself for a year.

DORIS Stop talking like a pair of maniacs. I've never heard so much damn twaddle. (*To Paul.*) And you, get a clean shirt on. You ain't going to school out of this house looking like a bloody drug addict. And I'm writing you a note, put you in the clear, if anybody did happen to see you coming home. (*Paul goes out. Doris gets up and rummages in the drawer for notepaper.*) Where's my notelets? (*She sits down at the table, and writes purposefully.*) "Dear Sir, Please excuse Paul's absence from school yesterday afternoon, as he was feeling ill due to a bilious turn." (*Licking down flap, she goes to the door, shouts upstairs to Paul.*) You've had a bilious turn. If they ask you, you've had a bilious turn . . . I've told 'em you've had a bilious turn.

GERRY You're overprotecting him, Doris. It ain't good for him.

DORIS I'm protecting his future. I ain't going to let that go west, say what you like. (*Winding gold cocktail watch.*) I'm going to send Madge a few flowers, I expect they took her up the General . . . you can drop me off when I get me cakes. Oo, my God, look at the time. We don't want to get on the wrong side of Fontaine. It's ten after eight.

GERRY Yeh, you don't want your name over the Tannoy for not being at your post when the whistle blows.

DORIS (*going out*) Yes, Elsie Green got three demerits last week for lateness . . . they told her if she gets any more, she'll be off piecework. (*She propels Gerry before her, and calls back to Paul:*) Paul, don't forget to drop this latch. And see you put that note in your pocket.

She goes out, gabbling instructions to Gerry.

Outside the Fontaine Production Centre

It is a long low building, with abundant fenestration and a central tower. The whole suggest a school, a clinic, a cinema, anything other than a factory. Doris and Gerry drive into the employees' car park—an area of rough broken asphalt adjacent to the Production Centre. There is a sticker in the back of their car:

"Face-Lift your World with Fontaine".

Gerry and Doris get out of the car. Doris slams her door, tries the lock, and then starts to run towards the factory entrance. She is clutching a large box of cakes. She stumbles on the uneven asphalt, and drops her cakes, some of which spill from the box. She scoops them up unceremoniously, blows the dust from them, and crams them back in the box. She resumes her run towards the employees' vestibule.

The vestibule

There is an unobtrusive clocking-in device. When the card is pushed in, a melodious chime registers.

Doris and Gerry arrive with one or two other stragglers.

Over the Tannoy comes the following message, strong regional accent with inflexion:

44

ANNOUNCER   Your Fontaine Goodmorning girl this week is Lynn Grayson,
and I am reminding you that the morning phase will commence
in thirty seconds' time, at eight-thirty. Special on the lunch-time
menu today is paella, with mango water-ice to follow. May I
remind late-comers that they forfeit their right to first sitting at
lunch.

The voice stops, and music takes its place.

DORIS   Oof, I damn near come a cropper on the asphalt then. Biggest
wonder out I never broke me ankle . . . (*To Gerry.*) get mine will
you Gerry at dinner-time, I might be a bit late. It's our turn in
the hall of perfumes this week to go and have our cervical
smear . . .

They separate through opposite rubberised flap-doors.

Doris's department

Doris at work in her department. All that is seen is a section of the work-line; two or three women flank Doris on either side. They are on high leatherette stools with back-rests. Suspended at eye-level is a serpentine intestinal arrangement of tubes and pipettes, through which courses an amber-coloured liquid, called Hint of Hibiscus. On a belt arrives a stream of simulated cut-glass flagons. The women raise the flagons to the automatic dispenser at the base of the tube, which spurts 17ccs of perfume into the flagon. It is then placed on another belt, which conveys it out of sight, to be stoppered. The action is quick and mechanical, requiring great motor deftness, but little use of any other human resources. The box of cakes lies beside Doris. In the background is music, distorted by the hum of machinery from other parts of the factory.

Doris is telling a joke; she is relaxed and ribald, as women are in female company, in contrast with her demeanour at home.

DORIS   . . . so the bloke says to her while he's getting dressed: "Thanks,
I enjoyed that," so the woman puts her eye back in, and the
bloke says, "I hope I'll see you again", and she says, "I'll keep
an eye out for you" . . .

(*laughter*)

FIRST WORKER   It's as old as the hills that one.

SECOND WORKER   You ought to stop telling stories like that Doris, now you're
forty-three.

DORIS   Who's forty-three? You're as old as you feel. And I feel a lot of
things, but old ain't one of 'em.

They all laugh.

THIRD WORKER   Here Doris, break your pipette today. I done mine yesterday,
I can't do it again. See if you can get that noo maintenance

45

feller round . . . that red-headed one.

DORIS What red-headed one?

FOURTH WORKER There's a noo 'un, ain't you seen him?

THIRD WORKER He don't half look something.

Laughter.

Gerry's department

Quality Control in the basic stores. A bare high room, stacked with raw materials: bell jars of liquid, crates of powder and grease. There are drums and containers of gum arabic, detergents, phials of vegetable extract, distilled essence of cardomum, jars of vaseline, etc. On a bench is an array of instruments for testing density, humidity, consistency, etc.

Gerry comes in, and puts on his white overalls that denote his technician's status. He is moody and disconsolate. There is one young man in the department, Ian, who is already working. They exchange unenthusiastic morning greetings. Gerry sits on a block of gypsum and lights a cigarette in calculated defiance of a "No Smoking" notice.

A Production Monitor looks in.

PROD. MONITOR What the bloody hell do you think you're doing? Put that fag out. I don't care if you blow yourself to kingdom come, but you ain't taking me with you. Three bags of powder came out of this room yesterday, with lumps in 'em as big as taters. It blocked up the dispensers, and it took half an hour to get them going again. Go on, get off that bloody block. You ain't in the tunnel of love. You're at work in case you've forgot what the bloody word means.

GERRY I ain't testing the stuff in them drums till they send some clean face-masks down. They should be here when we get in. I ain't sucking a hundredweight of talcum powder into me lungs for nobody, not without due and proper protection.

PROD. MONITOR Wouldn't hurt you to take five steps and go and fetch 'em yourself.

GERRY Yes it would, it'd hurt me a lot, 'cause it ain't my job.

PROD. MONITOR Oh ain't it? Who tells you it ain't? You do as you're told here, and the management does the telling, not some half-baked shop steward. You'll get your masks, then you won't have no excuses. (*Goes out, moaning.*) Bloody technicians, glorified office boys . . .

IAN Look, go and have your fag round the corner. We've got a nice little set-up here, we want to be left in peace. Soon as you start to step out of line they notice you.

GERRY (*contemptuous*) You. (*He sits down on the gypsum again, and lights up*

46

another cigarette.) Left in peace. Bloody grown man, wants to be left in peace. You're like a rat in a trap, and you think you're in clover.

IAN If this is a trap, I like being in it. I'm enjoying every minute of it as a matter of fact. I'm not short of a quid or two whenever I put me hand in me pocket, bit of minge in the recreation room if I feel the urge. I'm well-off here. You, you're all piss and vinegar. You want to relax and take what comes.

GERRY I bet they bloody love you here. You're just the sort of fodder they thrive on. You ain't got a thought in your head, you don't know where you've come from or where you're going. You'll wake up one morning and find it's all bin a bloody mirage. They'll be packed up and gone where they can get cheaper labour. You'll find yourself high and dry, no skills, no trade behind you, no nothing.

IAN I'll go with them then, won't I? I ain't here for life you know, like you. I'm going round the world before I settle down. Practise a few love positions in faraway places.

GERRY (*aggrieved and didactic*) I'll see you yet queuing up for public relief.

IAN I get plenty of relief thanks, as it is, but it's all in private.

GERRY You clevercock. Put your brains where your balls are, you'd use 'em more. (*Speaking to his workmate, who continues to work, conceding him only minimum attention.*) . . . I've had to sit at home when I was a kid, half past ten of a Saturday night, while our Mam went grubbing down the market, 'cause our old man was out of work . . . and we were grateful for a bit of cag-mag for Sunday dinner that somebody had chucked out . . . I had to cringe and whine for my first job, and do you know what it was when I got it? I had to go into the rough stuff room in Tarrant and Mercer's, before anybody got to work in the mornings, and empty the rat-traps. And at fifteen I got the sack, 'cause it was cheaper to employ another fourteen-year-old who'd just come out of school. Then I were out of work six months.

IAN Do you know what you are? You're a bloody crank. You can't get out of the past. I reckon you make all them stories up, about starving and being on the breadline.

GERRY If I'm a crank, it's cranks you owe all your easy living to now. I've seen stronger men than you reduced to breaking stones for the road for a few bob a day. You're feather-bedded against reality here. You've been conned. You walk about like a zombie. You've been taken over by the Fontaine mind-benders.

47

IAN I reckon you're a masochist. You really enjoyed all that, them dole queues and hard-hearted employers and landlords turning you out into the snow. You can't stand people being well-off and enjoying themselves. You glory in misery and doom. I don't know why you work here if you hate it so much.

GERRY Yes, I'll tell you why. (*Gets out union leaflets.*) Somebody's got to be here, see as they don't exploit bloody half-wits like you who think Fontaine dropped down from heaven just to shit little bits of toffee in your lap. . . .

There is a sullen resentful silence. They go half-heartedly about their work.

Walshs' office

Robert Walsh is at his desk with Personnel Manager. He is leafing through a wad of application forms.

ROBERT My God, they get worse every year . . . might as well stick a pin in the list . . . (*Reads.*) "Good executive material", what the bloody hell does he know about it? He's probably seen nothing but the inside of his school for forty years . . . (*Reads.*) "Brilliant but erratic". If he thinks that's any commendation to us he's got another think coming. . . . We ask the schools for reports, not this kind of tendentious claptrap . . . the whole system smacks of cloud cuckoo land . . . it's not scholarships they want: three years on the factory floor would give them a degree they won't get from college, a degree of practical experience . . . I don't like the idea of university scholarships. It's good for prestige, but they come under some pretty dubious influence once they get there. . . . Those we've sponsored so far have shown pretty poor return for all the money invested in them . . . bloody Standish, three years at eight hundred a year, and he stayed here two months and buggered off to ICI . . . he said we weren't employers, we were liege lords.

The Muddimans' front door

Doris and Gerry are just back from work. She picks up two letters from the mat.

DORIS (*in full spate*) . . . 'spect that'll mean another house for sale in the street before long. Madge looked after it though. She was born in that house . . . Ooo (*Expression of delight.*) I've got a card.

The kitchen—evening

DORIS Somebody's remembered me . . . Oo. It's from Fontaine. Lovely.

Picture of the Houses of Parliament . . . here, it's signed by Mr Merrick. (*Examining signature.*) I reckon he's signed it himself?

GERRY 'Course he ain't. They've got machines in the Visual Department, do Merrick's signature two hundred times a minute.

DORIS Go shut up you. Trust you to throw cold water on it. You couldn't even send me a card . . . there . . .
(*She puts it on the shelf.*) It says, "Greetings on your birthday. May God grant beauty with each passing day" . . . there . . .

GERRY It's the same card as last year.

DORIS No it's not. It said sommat different . . . I can't remember what it was, but it was different . . . means a rise . . . one forty-third of me wages, that's . . . er, about six bob a week. Mm, won't go far . . . here, here's a letter for Paul. Who's he getting letters from? Nice writing . . . (*Opens it.*) It's signed Madeleine. He don't know no Madeleines . . . has he got a girlfriend? (*Reads.*) Thursday's rehearsal cancelled. I must fly to town. Can you make it Friday instead? "Love, Madeleine." Madeleine Walsh that is. Sends her love. It's Madeleine now, they must be thick . . . (*Paul comes thundering in, in his school uniform.*)

PAUL What are you doing, opening my letters? They're private. That's mine. I don't touch yours.

DORIS Get away. You never have no letters.

PAUL Yes I do, that's one.

GERRY Bloody rehearsals. What does a factory want, doing drama?

DORIS I think it's a damn good idea, having a creative leisure scheme. Marvellous, keeps the youngsters off the streets. It'll smooth Paul's path with Fontaine. Looks good on an application form, that sort of thing.

PAUL You tamper with my mail again and I'll move into a flat on me own.

DORIS I hope you do everything Mrs Walsh tells you. She must be a clever woman.

PAUL I'll have a Post Office box number.

DORIS You keep in with her. She likes you. She might open doors for you.

GERRY Mind it ain't her bedroom door.

DORIS Shut up ignorant. (*To Paul.*) Mrs Walsh has been kindness itself to you. Play-acting gives you self-confidence, especially the lead. That's a real Christian act.

GERRY I don't know about her, but her husband's a reptile. Redhot Labour his people were one time of day. They slaved their guts out to keep him at college, and then he went straight over to the

49

other side and joined the management.

PAUL He's offered to give me driving lessons, so he can't be all that bad.

DORIS It's a privilege Paul, knowing them. You've got your foot in the door socially. You'll be round their house next. Managers' wives, I wouldn't a-dared open me mouth to her when I was your age. And here she is calling you by your first name and sending her love.

PAUL I'll be able to chat up all the right people once I get in with her.

GERRY (*contempt*) Chatting up the right people, hark at him. (*Sententious.*) There ain't no such thing as the right people in this world. There's only good people and bad people, and most of them the Walshes know are bloody shockers.

PAUL (*sees the cards*) Oh, it's her birthday.

DORIS Who's her? Her ain't here, but your mother is. I think it's a scandal, neglect your mother's birthday. Not that I want anything from you, cause I don't, the pair of you.

PAUL Oh, we forgot.

DORIS Yes, and I might just forget to come home one of these days. Ain't it all right, eh? I ain't allowed to forget you two one single day of the year, but you ain't got a spark of feeling between you. Not that I want gifts, cause I don't, but you might a managed a token.

GERRY Don't holler before you're hurt, Doris. How do you know I ain't saving up to get you sommat nice at the weekend?

DORIS What's it going to be then, a silver new-nothing-at-all?
Gerry goes and places his arms round her shoulders conciliatingly. She shakes them off.

GERRY I'm going to buy you that trouser suit you tried on in Fairbrother. You said it made you wish you was a teenager, so I thought well, let her feel like one, she'll never look like one again.

DORIS Don't soft soap me . . . you've only just thought that one up ain't you? . . . Still, (*Reflective.*) it'd sit as well on me as anybody. I'll hold you to that, Harry . . . and Paul's a witness. Did you hear that Paul? . . . Yes, we can go down tomorrow morning and put a deposit on it . . . that'll be an eye-opener for'em at the Fontaine Family Day do . . .

GERRY I don't mind buying you a new outfit for your birthday, but I'm not buying it for Fontaine's benefit.

DORIS Fontaine's benefited you enough one way or another. Same as it has all of us . . . Fontaine's been a godsend to me, without a word of a lie.

50

GERRY I happen to know, their women workers in America get three times what you do. To them we're cheap labour.

DORIS Didn't stop you crowing over your pay-packet this evening!

The vestibule

It is Fontaine Family Day, and they are waiting for the coach. There is anticipation and excitement.

Doris and Gerry, Paul, Rose and her husband, and some of the workers from Doris's department with their men.

IAN Where's our coach?

GERRY *(morose)* 'Spect it's had a breakdown.

DORIS *(sharp)* I shall have a bloody breakdown if you start. Whittleguts you are: you ain't putting the kybosh on my day out, so pipe-down.

IAN Get with it Gerry, you can milk 'em to some tune today. All them free drinks, six-course dinner. Should've thought it was up your street.

DORIS Here, there goes Lips and Eyes. We shall be last ... look, they've got wind-up headrests on their coach.

ROSE Here, that Doll Tuckley, did you see who she's got in tow with her? If that's her husband, she's changed him since last year. They'll go mad if they find out she's brought someone as ain't a relation.

DORIS *(nudging Rose)* The only relations she has are sexual ones.
Laughter.

BILL *(affable)* Here, mind your language, you ain't on the pipettes now Rose. Innocent men and boys might be listening.

ROSE That lets you out then, Bill, dunnit?

GERRY Damn ridic'lous, splitting everybody up like this. Why can't we all go to the same place, like last year. Wasn't bad that.

ROSE No, it was them ignorant sods from Packing last year. They bust all them windows at the road-house. Cost Fontaine a mint.

DORIS There's always somebody got to go and spoil things, ain't there.

BILL Here it comes.

DORIS Come on, Paul.

PAUL I don't wanner come.

ROSE *(sharp)* What's up, Paul? Ain't we good enough for yer now?

DORIS Come on. Gerry, you got them oranges?

GERRY Is that the bloody bus? I thought it was scrap iron. I 'spect they've tinkered with the engine, so's we all go crashing to our deaths. Save 'em a few quid in redundancy pay.

DORIS *(with a gesture of hopeless resignation to Rose)* How should you want to live with that, Rose? It's the same day and night. He don't let up for a minute.

The coach comes juddering to a halt. They scramble to get on, all pushing, while pretending not to.

DORIS *(to a man who is about to get on)* Ladies first. *(She elbows him aside.)*

Inside the bus

Gerry is sitting with one of the other men, looking mournful and un-festive. He addresses his companion rarely, and then only with information, e.g. as they pass a large tree, he says:

GERRY That used to be a hanging tree years agoo. Not many people realise that. They used to hang people by the dozen in them days.

His companion pays no attention.

This is a contrast with Doris and Rose. They are talking in low voices, Rose relaying a piece of scandal, Doris agog.

ROSE Didn't you see it? One of the women that cleans the offices got hold of it, and she passed it all round the canteen one dinner-time.

DORIS No, what did it say?

ROSE Well, it was from this woman who'd written to Fontaine to complain about their toilet soap. And what she wrote was, "I lost a bar of Lemon Verbena in the bath. And as it could not have gone down the plughole I conclude that I must have lost it about my person. Should I seek medical advice concerning this matter?" *(Doris doesn't catch on for a moment: then shrieks with laughter.) Then recovers, and peers through the headrest to the seat at the back.)* Here, Doll, did you hear that? It's the best yet. . . .

Paul is looking unhappy and embarrassed.

A pub restaurant

A spacious pub restaurant. Brasses, Spanish ironwork, red lamp-shades, display of superior plastic flowers.

There is a painted window with a view of the Matterhorn, and fake beams and leaded windows, calculated to create the kind of atmosphere vaguely felt to be traditional and English.

Gerry, Rose and her husband Bill and Ian seated round a table. Paul is on the end, looking left out.

There is a general atmosphere of mild inebriety. Around the bar is a thick crush. A whistle blows to indicate the end of free drinks.

From the throng Doris disengages herself, carrying three glasses pre-cariously in each hand. Doris joins the others at the table.

DORIS (*triumphant*) I got 'em just as the whistle went . . . I was the last one to get 'em for nothing, anything you have from now on you pay for. . . . Some clumsy herbert spilt half his pale ale down me blouse . . . I've got like a wet clammy feeling all down me front.

GERRY I think it's degrading to see human beings sinking all that liquor in half an hour, just cos it's free.

DORIS You're drinking enough of it . . . you're well on the way to being kalied . . . here Rose, I got a whiff of what's cooking at the bar. We ain't half in for a feed . . . I seen 'em taking a tray of shrimp cocktails through. I said to him "Are they for us?" D'you know what he said? "No, I'm just taking them for their daily walk."

ROSE I'm starving, and if Bill don't get his grub in him, he starts blowing orf like a storm at sea . . .

BILL It was that operation I had . . .

ROSE Nobody wants to hear your ailments.

GERRY (*sententiously*) Doris, me duck, happiness don't begin and end with a shrimp cocktail.

ROSE If I'm lucky I might get another sort of shrimp cocktail before tonight's out. What's the chances Bill?

BILL If I can't get orf with Doris I might consider it.

DORIS (*flattered*) You cheeky bugger. Can you hear what your husband's saying, Rose?

BILL We'll have a wife-swapping. How about it Gerry?

GERRY Swap her? I'd bloody well give her away.

BILL You'll be all right, Doris. D'you know what Fontaine are cooking up next?

DORIS No, what?

BILL Love Potion. Dab of that and he'll be running round.
There are shrieks of laughter.

ROSE Here, that's enough of that, you.

BILL That's right though. They reckon there's a big market for it.

DORIS How they goin' to make it then?

ROSE Be all right is they spilt it in the factory. There'd be an orgy.

GERRY I reckon we live in a society that's gone sex-mad.

IAN Yes, and ain't it nice?

GERRY I don't believe in sweeping it under the carpet, don't run away with that idea, but you're come to a poor pass when you can't talk about nothing else on a day out.

DORIS (*ignoring him*) How does it work then, Bill?

BILL What?

DORIS This love-potion. There's no such thing.

IAN   I know there is. Natives use em. They make it out of tropical plants.

DORIS   Here, Rose, guess what they'd got on the market yesterday? They was selling Venus fly-traps. They're tropical.

ROSE   What do they do then?

DORIS   They catch flies.

GERRY   People ain't got minds of their own, they're all the while got to be titillated.

ROSE   Who's being dirty, now? (*Laughter, then a lull*). Look, there's Jean lickin' her chops like the cat that got the cream . . . who's that bloke with her? . . . (*They all turn round*). Don't look, they'll see you . . . he's somebody out of management.

DORIS   He'll be lucky if he can manage her.

ROSE   You know, Jean, you raise my salary, I'll raise my skirts.
There is laughter, which freezes as Robert and Madeleine Walsh appear by the table. They rise, raggedly, except Gerry.

ROBERT   (*affably*) No, no, don't get up . . . mind if we join you?

GERRY   (*disagreeably under his breath*) Why, are we coming to pieces?

ROBERT   May I present my wife, Madeleine?
Madeleine recognises Paul, and exchanges a smile.

ROSE   Madeleine, that's my favourite name. If I'd had a girl I was gunner call her Madeleine.

DORIS   I'm Mrs Muddiman, Paul's mother. He talks ever so highly of you . . . it's bin real help to him doing drama. It gives them confidence . . .

ROSE   Kevin's going in for the Fontaine Scholarship.

DORIS   So's Paul.

ROBERT   May we sit down?

DORIS   Yes, you sit here, hotch up Gerry.

ROBERT   Well I don't need to ask whether you're enjoying yourselves. Just to hear the laughter coming from this table makes the whole day worth while. . . .

DORIS   Ooo, were we making too much noise, Mr Walsh? I'm ever so sorry.

ROBERT   Not at all. Quite the reverse. We don't want any spectres at the feast.

BILL   This'll give a boost to productivity, Mr Walsh.

ROBERT   Yes. Yes . . . I suppose it will. Not what it's intended for of course, ha, ha.
There is an awkward silence.

DORIS   I expect you find all these do's very boring, Mrs Walsh?

MADELEINE   No, no. I find them fascinating.

54

GERRY   It shows you how the workers enjoy themselves, dunnit?

ROBERT   I think we all enjoy ourselves in the same way. Enjoyment is pretty much of a muchness everywhere I think.

IAN   Will you have a drink, Mr Walsh?

ROBERT   That is extraordinarily kind of you, but I must refuse . . . I've already drunk rather a lot, and I have to drive back.

GERRY   'Spect coach travel makes you feel sick.
         There is another silence.

DORIS   That's a lovely dress, Mrs Walsh.

MADELEINE I'll tell you a secret about it. I bought it in the British Home Stores.

DORIS   Ooo. I say. Did you hear that, Rose? British Home Stores.

ROSE   Yes. Lovely material.
         Again silence for a fraction of a second longer than is socially appropriate.

ROBERT   (*jovially*) You must have been telling each other some pretty spicy stories . . . surely you've got one left for me?
         They giggle a little.

MADELEINE I really must have a word with your morose son, Mrs Muddiman.
         She gets up and sits beside Paul on the other side of him so they form a separate group.

ROBERT   And I'll have to mingle . . . ha, ha. Six times a day. Very good.

MADELEINE (*calls as Robert goes*) I'll be with you in a moment darling. (*The main group reverts to relaxed laughter. Madeleine speaks to Paul confidentially.*) God it's awful, isn't it?

PAUL   It's horrible.

MADELEINE Why on earth did you come?

PAUL   Mum said I ought to because of the Fontaine Scholarship. She says it'll look better if I attend all Fontaine's functions.

MADELEINE Oh, I see now why you joined the Fontaine Players.

PAUL   I don't care about the scholarship.

MADELEINE Oh but you must. Robert tells me there are twenty-three applicants, but on the whole they're a dreary lot. . . . We had one or two of them at the Ranch House last year, they were so boring. One of them even asked if I knew the chemical properties of Hint of Hibiscus. They were all owlish and inarticulate scientists. Ghastly.

PAUL   I'm not really a scientist . . . my mother used to call me the inventor and the professor ever since I can remember. It was just a foregone conclusion . . . I'm still doing one Arts subject though. I'm doing French. But I shan't get it, I'm only doing two periods a week and I don't even know what the set books are.

MADELEINE Books should never be set. It makes them sound like blanc-mange. I used to loathe set books when I was teaching. All those dreary girls demanding notes, notes, notes all the time, as if I were some kind of warbler. . . . I used to tell them, "Read the book over and over, and then just respond to it".

PAUL I can't imagine you teaching.

MADELEINE I did two terms. The school was frightful . . . any inclination I had towards pedagogy was smothered by starchy food and excessive emotionalism. Teaching is quite nice, but schools are vile. Would you like me to teach you some French?

PAUL Eh? . . . Are you qualified to . . . ?

MADELEINE I have a degree, which is utterly meaningless of course. Well . . . shall I teach you? I'll give you a few lessons if you like.

PAUL Euh . . . (*Embarrassed.*) . . . I don't think they could afford it.

MADEELINE I wouldn't do it for money, silly . . . it would help me not to atrophy intellectually. My brain is in danger of withering away in Litchborough. A few lessons would give it a jolt.

PAUL I wouldn't dare talk French in front of you, I'm awful.

MADELEINE I'll do the talking then, and you can repeat what I say. Come over to the Ranch House on Friday and we can talk about it. You know Castle Chase? It's the first house inside the Lodge Gates.

PAUL (*overwhelmed*) I'll come on me bike . . . thanks . . .

MADELEINE I must go and find Robert now. A tout a l'heure . . . (*She goes.*)

DORIS (*eagerly leaning across to Paul*) What did she say to you, Paul?

PAUL She offered to give me some help with my French.

ROSE (*acrimoniously*) Help you with your French what?

DORIS Rose, he needs his French. Is she going to give you lessons?

PAUL She used to live in Paris.

ROSE Oo, la la!

GERRY We ain't paying her good money for lessons when you go to a state school. If they can't teach you, it must mean you're too thick to learn.

PAUL It's not for money.

GERRY For what then?

PAUL For nothing.

DORIS She wants to help him . . . that sort of people, they can make a gesture like that . . . (*Getting up.*) . . . I'd better go after her and thank her. . . .

PAUL Sit down, Mum. . . .

GERRY Where's she reckon she's goin' to teach you? She ain't coming to our house is she?

PAUL   No, I'm going to her.

DORIS (*triumphantly*) There Rose, what do you think to that?

ROSE   I can think what I bloody well like, can't I?

DORIS You're well in now, Paul.

GERRY (*aggrieved*) Are we his bloody parents or is she? Don't consult us will you, we only brought him up . . . comes dinxing in here, grinning like a bloody death's head, and you all start fawnin' on her . . . it's disgusting. (*To Paul.*) She can bloody well adopt you if she likes you that much.

DORIS Oh, Gerry. (*Weary.*) He's got to the argumentative stage. For Christ's sake have another so's we can lay you out on the back seat of the coach or else sober up. . . .

IAN   (*ironically*) Paul, you must be a big disappointment to your Dad, going over to the management . . . bit of a come-down for Gerry the Red.

GERRY We had a word for that in our lectures in 1948. Class-traitor.

DORIS Don't talk clap-trap, Gerry.

       A whistle blows. There is a sudden activity.

DORIS That's the dinner whistle, goo on Rose, you prop him up, and I'll goo and collar us a table near the window. Come on, get your skates on, don't want no other buggers tealeafing our shrimp cocktail.

       There is a general rush towards the dining-room.

Walshs' office

       A knock at the door.

ROBERT (*tetchily*) Yes?

       The Production Monitor's head appears round the door; he is deferential.

PROD. MONITOR Are you busy, Mr Walsh, 'cause I'd like a word with you if you've got five minutes. . . .

ROBERT Five minutes, I never have five seconds, come in, come in.

PROD. MONITOR Thanks ever so much, Mr Walsh . . . (*He is embarrassed.*)

ROBERT Yes, yes?

PROD. MONITOR I'm had sommat on me mind the last two days . . . I'm worried. . . . Matter of fact I'm bin losing sleep over it, and you're the only one as can set me mind at rest.

ROBERT Sit down . . . I'm sure it's nothing we can't hammer out between us . . . (*A new contrived jocularity.*) Spill the beans, Eric.

PROD. MONITOR Well . . . it's about you know who . . . Lenin's on the warpath again.

ROBERT Ah. Mm. (*Uncertain.*)

PROD. MONITOR Gerry the Red, Muddiman. . . he can't leave people to get on with the job; he's gotter be all the while at them about needing a union. I told him I said they need a union like they need a hole in the head . . . but he won't let 'em be, he had a pile of pamphlets from the Transport and General on Monday. He was only dishing them out in work time.

ROBERT   I see . . . he knows Fontaine's philosophy . . . the family looks after its own . . . when the family has a difference of opinion you don't run out and fetch a policeman. . . . (*Significant pause.*) Is anybody . . . listening to him?

PROD. MONITOR   Well there's one or two of the lads, youngsters as 've only just fell out of bed, want a lark, they'd follow anybody as promised 'em a bit of rough-house. . . . You know what he was saying on the Family Day outing? He said "We ain't men, we're Fontaine powder puffs".

ROBERT   We'll keep tabs on him. Might do him good to cool his heels in the labelling room.

PROD. MONITOR   Yis, but that ain't the all of it, not by a yard and a half. . . . Tain't only what he says . . . he's come damn near industrial sabotage once or twice this week.

ROBERT   Oh? . . . That's a very grave accusation . . . are you sure you mean sabotage?

PROD. MONITOR   Well not sabotage p'raps, but serious disruption. . . . Yesterday, when the good ladies from Zone 417 was being shown round . . . he disconnected the crude talc supply pipe. It blew the powder all over the show. It was like the Sahara in there for five minutes.

ROBERT   Now this is serious. Political agitation is harmless, but we're not going to tolerate that kind of tomfoolery .. . . You do have evidence do you, that he deliberately disconnected the pipe?

PROD. MONITOR   Well I never seen him . . . but that's never happened once in all my ten years here . . . it must 'a bin deliberate. And you should have seen the way he was smirking, it took me all my time to keep my hands off him. . . .

ROBERT   Mm . . . well I think we've got enough to get moving on this one now. Thank you very much indeed for being so . . . vigilant . . . I've never known anyone have cause to regret his loyalty to Fontaine.

PROD. MONITOR   Thank you Mr Walsh. . . . Er . . . er . . . (*He is reluctant to go on.*) Mr Walsh, there is one thing . . .

ROBERT   Yes?

PROD. MONITOR   I had this idea . . . for a name . . . for the competition . . . for the competition for product names . . . I were going to put it in the suggestions box, but I thought I'd ask your opinion about it first . . . the wife asked me to have a word with you, it was her idea really . . .

ROBERT   Yes, yes.

OD.MONITOR   It's Jessamine Water. Jessamine Water . . . and I'll tell you where it comes from. We went on holiday, and we was passing this villa on the bus, Jessamine Villa it were called, and she said, "How about Jessamine for a name for the competition?" But I didn't think it was worth entering, so she said—

ROBERT   Oh yes, I think it's very felicitous. Very felicitous indeed. I like it. Tell you what I'll do. I'll by-pass the suggestions box and pass it straight on to Promotions and Creativity. . . .

OD.MONITOR   Oo thank you. Mr Walsh . . . that's very kind of you. Hilda will be pleased . . . well . . . er . . . duty calls.

ROBERT   Yes, yes. And thank you for coming. (*The Production Monitor goes out. Robert turns on the dictaphone.*) Memo to Personnel: "File Number 2,734. Muddiman G., Rectification. Obstructionist. Evidence of agitation. Appears to be meeting with very little success. Also query hooliganism. There now appear to be grave doubts as to this man's dependability." God there's all this to get out today . . . this West Africa contract. If we're going to back up this new skin bleach with sales literature, we're going to have to get some coloured models . . . we shall need full-blooded Negro ladies for the before shots, and some half-castes for the shots after the course of treatment . . . mm . . . tricky . . . race relations bill . . . it'll mean an advert in the trade papers. . . . Mm . . . Octoroons wanted . . . (*Chuckles.*)

Inside Doris's department

DORIS   Oo yis, Paul gets on ever so well with both of them him and her. Oo, they have been good to him. Who else would give him French lessons for nothing? On the day out, she offered, you was there wasn't you, Rose?

ROSE   He's a real trier. He's got as good a chance of getting the scholarship as anybody, without going in for all this drama business.

DORIS   Well, it's bin heaven-sent to our Paul, because Mr Walsh turns out to be one of the big-wigs on the selection committee.

ROSE   Oo, well, if Paul's dancing attendance on them every minute of the day and night, what chance are ordinary folks got?

DORIS   Well, you know what they say about your Keith at school, they say his one O Level a year's an annual event. Damn. Damn pipette ain't spurting straight. . . .

The patio of the Walshs' house

A corner of the patio in the Walshs' ranch house. It is evening. There are two elegant wrought-iron chairs, a table and a tinkling mobile above. A jug of lemonade with glass ladle. Madeleine histrionic—provincial grande dame and exiled graduate. She is in a cool silk dress with a chiffon scarf. She wears a heavy bracelet, ornately wrought metal, studded with garnets. Paul is present. There is a languid disabused coquetry in her manner.

MADELEINE . . . Il etait d'ailleurs syphilitique, et il est mort dans des circonstance saffreuses . . . il s'est sacrifié pour la poesie. . . . You see, Paul, his poetry was his life. He tried to find escape from reality in all kinds of experience and debauchery. He was the first of the moderns. . . . This whole modern thing really began with Baudelaire, so I really don't see why they make such a fuss about drug-taking and all that kind of thing.

PAUL *(impressed)* I wish you could come and teach at our school, Mrs Walsh.

MADELEINE *(archly)* Mrs Walsh! *(Mock cross.)* You know, Paul, it's you young people who create the generation gap. I've asked you to call me Madeleine, but you go on talking to Mrs Walsh, who's an entirely different person. . . . It's really most trying.

PAUL Sorry . . . Madeleine, it's just a habit you get into at school. Why don't you come and teach though?

MADELEINE I should enjoy it immensely, Paul, but unfortunately it's just not possible for directors' wives to work. My function is simply to be decorative and charming to overseas buyers. Most of the time I sit around feeling sorry for myself because so much of Robert's life is taken up by the all-engulfing Fontaine.

PAUL I can't imagine anybody feeling sorry for themselves in a place like this. I mean, you mix with a lot of people, a lot of interesting people come here.

MADELEINE A lot of people come here full stop. But they couldn't be more boring if they tried. Litchborough people are so parochial. Their social life consists of sitting in each other's houses returning cutlet for cutlet at regular monthly intervals.

PAUL Yes, I don't think I could bear to live here. Not when I've been to university and got sophisticated.

MADELEINE Well, I hope you'll come and see me sometime. The trouble is that Robert's life is inextricably involved with Fontaine. We may have to moulder here on eight thousand a year for ever.

PAUL You don't moulder. You do so many things in the town. Even our English teacher says you've given new life to the arts club.

60

MADELEINE Well I have to do something to prove I'm not simply an append-age of my husband. And even running that takes up only a minute portion of my time and energy. It's really rather grue-some, trying to arrange guest speakers for schoolteachers and library assistants who turn into artists and visionaries after dark. . . . The slim volume they're writing gets slimmer every year as their waists get proportionately fatter.

PAUL At least they're willing to talk about literature and books. My mother, the only book she's ever read all through is *Peyton Place*. I have to go and get it out of the library every time she has the flu. Apart from that, *Fontaine News* is the limit of her acquaintance with the printed word.

The Muddimans' kitchen

Doris and Gerry are at home. Gerry is washing up after tea. Doris is flicking through the 'Fontaine News'.

DORIS (*reads*) "This month's birthdays . . . " They've spelt my name wrong. Muddiman, only one d. That'd make it Moodiman.

GERRY (*sarcastic*) Fontaine takes a personal interest. Fontaine's com-puters take a personal interest. The only personal interest they take is in how much of their goods you're trying to smuggle out through the gates. Fontaine keeps a friendly eye on you, only trouble is it's an electric one.

DORIS (*ignoring him, and going on reading*) Ooo, that Janice who works in Talcum, she's got engaged . . . Ooo, to the bloke who was man-ager of Campaign thirty-six. (*Reads.*) "The Fontaine Cupid has been busy again. We think it must be something irresistible in our Fontaine Moondust that sweeps three girls into romance and matrimony in three short months. Latest victim of Cupid's quiver is dishy Janice Carter, who claims Big Jim Green, of Marketing Strategy. Let's hope sales don't fall off after the happy day." All the girls at Fontaine have got their eye on some chap or other in management. They're just the same on the pipettes, them as ain't married. Some of them as are an' all . . . I hope they don't goo making a beeline for our Paul when he gets there. We want somebody a bit better 'n that for him—

GERRY Good God, Doris, he's only flesh and blood. If he wants to marry some nice decent little gal I shouldn't stop him

DORIS You're dripping soap all over the floor. How many times 've I told you to keep them dishes over the sink? . . . We ain't sacrificed all we have for him to get snapped up by some smart little madam in the Talcum Department. College is the place to meet girls for somebody of Paul's calibre.

GERRY You've got it all too pat Doris. If I was him, I'd run away and join the Merchant Navy. I wouldn't let anybody map my future out. They talk about rebellious youth. This one does a damn sight too much of what he's told. If that Mrs Walsh told him to go and jump in the river he'd do it. That firm, I reckon they run this house by remote control. You're a robot Doris, a human robot. I'm fed up with being a Fontaine zombie, I reckon I'll pack it in.

DORIS Don't talk tripe, Gerry.

The Walshs' patio

PAUL They want me to get on, but you can't talk to them about anything. My mother's always done her best for me. I mean, she respects the education I'm getting. (*Confidentially.*) . . . It's ever so funny, she treats my books as if they were so fragile she daren't pick them up . . . she's houseproud really, but she never moves my books, even if I've left them all over the place. She says, "They're Paul's books, I won't touch them, I'll just dust around them." But she hasn't got the faintest idea what's in them.

MADELEINE I wouldn't condemn anybody who hasn't read, especially if they've been at an educational disadvantage. But when one's with them, one's always conscious of it

PAUL Yes, they can't communicate can they?

MADELEINE Yes dear, but you must remember, there are other ways of communicating. For instance, if I touch your hand . . . (*She places her hand on his and leaves it there.*) That's a form of communication. (*He tries to pull away.*) No. You see, I knew you'd draw away. Just sit still and see if you can feel what I'm trying to communicate. (*He now draws his hand away.*) Really! (*Pettishly.*) English people are so embarrassed by physical contact. I'm the kind of person who, if I love someone I want to kiss them, and if I hate them I want to hit them. . . . But most people, for some unaccountable reason, find it more convenient to be hypocritical to each other, and hide what they really feel. For instance, now, now, what are you thinking? You won't tell me will you?

PAUL Yes, I was wondering how much this house cost to build.

MADELEINE (*silvery laugh*) There. I knew you wouldn't tell me. (*Serious.*) That's not the truth is it?

PAUL Yes, it is.

MADELEINE Then I'm very insulted. I sit here, holding your hand, and all the time you're wondering how much my house cost. You're being a true son of Litchborough, and I don't want to talk to you any more.

PAUL I wasn't really thinking that, Madeleine.

MADELEINE No, of course you weren't.

PAUL I was thinking how boring I must be to you.

MADELEINE Boring? What makes you think that?

PAUL Well I must be. All those people at that party last Saturday . . . they kept asking me where I'd been and what I'd done. I've bin to Jersey twice and I've done half me A levels and that's it.

MADELEINE Yes darling, but you're so much more intelligent than any of them. It doesn't matter where they've been, they're the kind of people who would turn Katmandu into a suburb of Litchborough. I hope you don't confuse me with them.

PAUL Oh no. I think you're fantastic, the way you can handle people. I could never have done what you did at the party. The way you walked across the room to that woman who was screeching and swearing, and just slapped her face . . .

The Muddimans' kitchen

DORIS (*she reads*) Says here that Fontaine Family Day for next year will be on the 12th July. Oo, I did enjoy meself last Toosday—I died o' laughing. That Mr Walsh, you can really talk to him, he ain't got a scrap of side on him. There will be a trip to the heart of the Shakespeare Country for all Fontaine employees, in commemoration of Mrs Henriette Weismuller, Mother of Fontaine. There. That'll be a real occasion, a dinner banquet to follow. A banquet. Not just a dinner . . .

GERRY I shall be left by then.

DORIS What?

GERRY I shall be left.

DORIS Left behind is about all you'll be. You're talking half sharp, Gerry. How could you leave with all we've got at stake through them?

GERRY I look through the paper every night, keep an eye open.

DORIS You're just trying to get at me and Paul ain't yer? Leaving, you no more thought of leaving than you thought of sprouting wings and flying over the Windermere Estate.

GERRY You've turned this house into an annexe of the Hall of bloody Perfumes. I don't want to stand here and listen to you chopsing about Fontaine and all their propaganda.

They fall into silence. She flicks through the magazine. Gerry finishes the dishes.

The Walshs' patio

MADELEINE   ... I'm sure it's working in that oppressively feminine atmosphere that makes all the men so anxious to prove their virility. It's a rutting shop. Horrible.

PAUL   You don't think of all that going on in a factory, do you?

MADELEINE   Don't let them hear you call it a factory; it's a production centre. Anyway, now we're both being boring. Fontaine seeps into everyone. It pervades the whole atmosphere, like their evil-smelling products. I won't let Robert come near me until he's changed his suit after work. It's worse than tear gas. It makes my eyes stream. They ought to sell the formula to the Ministry of Defence.

PAUL   (*laughing*) You put me right off. I shall never be able to work for Fontaine after I've got my degree.

MADELEINE   I should hope not. But for God's sake, don't let Robert hear you say so or he won't sponsor you. . . . Robert's anxious to promote only people who show signs of the same religious dedication to business that he's possessed by. For him selling and commerce are the only real human activities. He's always on about the rough and tumble of the market place.

PAUL   I think I might be an actor when I finish college. I don't think I care about money, Madeleine. I used to, it used to matter to me a lot. I think self-expression's more important.

MADELEINE   Mm? Well, darling, your range is a tiny bit narrow at the moment. After all, the only theatre you've done is a few re-hearsals of "Boy" in "Hot Wind from the Delta". You're not quite groomed for the Comédie Française.

PAUL   I've made fantastic progress under your direction, Madeleine . . . I can talk from the diaphragm now. I was going to ask you though, when it says in the stage directions "Controlled hysteria" when he's asking Rosalia if she wants a mint julep, well I mean, I don't think you can be controlled and have hysteria at the same time.

MADELEINE   I told you to ignore all the printed directions. Just listen to what I say and try to respond. What I would like to do, if you haven't got to dash off, is just look at that seduction scene between Boy and Rosalia.

PAUL   Yes we are a bit under-rehearsed, because Barbara always has to go early for her Commerce Class at Tech.

MADELEINE   I'll read Rosalia . . . just go through the last bit, from where she says, "Very soon a hot wind will rise . . . ". (*She reaches for a copy of "Hot Wind from the Delta", scored heavily with notes and directions.*)

64

Now then . . . (*She pushes aside the chairs. She starts reading histrionically and lyrically.*) "Very soon a hot wind will rise and I'll go all round the house closin' the shutters and pulling down the blinds . . . it'll be dark in here. And cool. So cool. . . . "

PAUL "I love the hot wind, it's like a caress."

MADELEINE (*own voice*) Paul, you say it as if you're reading from the Acts of the Apostles in morning assembly. Try again. You're agitated because I'm making love to you.

PAUL (*with somewhat more inflexion*) "I love the hot wind, it's like a caress."

MADELEINE (*sighs*) "I don't know what a caress is like, it's bin so long. . . . "

PAUL "You mustn't talk like that Rosalia, you're too beautiful. . . . You're beautiful like a summer's day is beautiful, but you can't possess a summer's day."

MADELEINE "Can a summer's day kiss?" (*Own voice.*) No, darling. Paul stand still, I'm not carnivorous . . . when you're kissed on stage you turn your head away and let the other person do the work. (*Rosalia voice.*) "Your lips are cold, Boy. Why? Why are they cold when mine are so warm?"

PAUL "You can taste death on them Rosalia, that's why they're cold . . . " (*Own voice.*) Daft, Madeleine. I can't say that in front of people . . . nobody I know talks like that.

MADELEINE (*in her own voice; silvery, relaxed*) You do it beautifully, darling. It's the stupidest play I've ever heard; you're quite right.
She throws her fichu round his neck and knots it, and she kisses him lightly on the nose. He is frozen with embarrassment.

The Muddimans' kitchen

Paul comes in, carrying his books and a copy of the play, and wearing Madeleine's fichu. Paul, good-humoured, sits down in chair, sprawling.

DORIS Did you learn all your French?

PAUL You don't learn with Madeleine. You just soak it in.

GERRY So does a bloody sponge. What's that rag doing round your neck.

PAUL It's not doing anything, it's just there.

GERRY Take it orf. You look damn ridiculous.

DORIS I think it suits him. Tain't a nancy colour. Boys can take that kind of thing these days.

GERRY What other of her clothes did you put on?

DORIS Don't be low you.

PAUL She's really generous, giving me these lessons for nothing. She could charge thirty bob an hour. I learn more from her in a

65

couple of hours than I do in a whole term at school. She was a teacher at one time. Fantastic house, Mum. There's three bathrooms. They have a fire in a pit.

GERRY So does hell.

PAUL In the middle of the room. There's a sunken conversation area, so the room's on different levels. It's like a stage set.

DORIS You're a privileged boy, Paul.

GERRY Yes he is, bloody privileged, if what they say at work is anything to go by.

DORIS We don't want none of your dirty men's talk at home if you don't mind.

GERRY It's common knowledge what she's after, and she ain't getting it from my son.

PAUL (*furious*) You repulsive ignorant pig. (*Sobbing anger.*) She's bloody fabulous . . . and sensitive . . . and intelligent. (*Running off upstairs slamming the door.*) Something you don't know anything about in this house.

Doris goes after him, and calls upstairs.

DORIS Paul . . . Paul . . . (*No response. She turns back into the room.*) You can damage growing boys with that sort of talk, specially if they're brainy . . . he's got enough on his plate with these exams, and he ain't got to be upset. The doctor said he's incapable of giving his maximum performance through nerves. . . .

GERRY It's your fault. You've reaped your reward, putting it about that we're thick as thieves with the Walshes. Everybody thinks he's up every night, the way you're blarting about it. They think he goes up to the Ranch House for one bloody reason, and we aid and abet.

DORIS I don't want to hear a word of gossip from any of them. Gerry, if you ain't got the sense to see that's envy talking, you're a poor fish. Envy makes ugly noises, and always has done. (*She goes upstairs to Paul.*) Paul . . . come on, you come and tell me all about the Walshes house . . .

Doris's department at the factory

Doris is on the pipettes. She is jaunty and knowing. She is singing "You may not be an angel." (Pause while she works.) "But all the same you'll do" (Pause.) "And until the day one comes along (pause) I'll string along with you." Then she la-la's the next verse. Rose keeps looking at her. Doris is aware of her scrutiny.

ROSE I know what she's squawking about, before she opens her mouth

FIRST WORKER Yis, she's opened her front parlour for some reason or other.

(*They laugh.*)

FOURTH WORKER That right Doris?

DORIS Good God, gal, I'm too old to cry roast meat at my age.

FOURTH WORKER Well sommat's put the joys of spring in yer.

ROSE I know what's happened. Her Paul. He's got the scholarship.

THIRD WORKER That right, Doris?

DORIS I known a fortnight. We only had the letter to confirm it this morning. D'you wanna see it? (*She passes round the letter.*)

ROSE I wouldn't want Keith tied to Fontaine. He wants his freedom. He wouldn't want to come back to Litchborough, not when he's been to college.

DORIS Oo, Paul'll go straight to the top of the tree. It'll be an open sesame . . . I reckon the school'll cough up to a fair tune, they do when they get scholarships, there's a grant for this, a grant for the other. . . .

ROSE You wanna try givin' us a grant duck, grant us a bit of peace and quiet about it.

THIRD WORKER What's it worth Doris?

DORIS Well, this is hundred and fifty clear, no strings. But it guarantees his place at college in Nottingham. . . . It ain't got to go through the channels. But you ain't heard the best part of it, we're got an invitation, me and Gerry and all. We're all going over to the Ranch House, written invitation we're got. We're going for our dinner. Evenin'. They're givin' a bit of a celebration in Paul's honour. They're lovely people. When I hear folks callin 'em, it makes me see red. They've treated our Paul handsome. Mr Walsh even gave him driving lessons. Mr Walsh says it's give and take these days, it's not the old boss running the firm. They're doing a job of work same as we are. He says it don't make sense to squabble. The hands don't quarrel with the head do they?

ROSE Don't quote him at me, the dirty ole sod. Know how he got hold of that young gal who calls herself his secretary? He looked round the lipstick cartridge room one day and picked her out. And she can't hardly spell her own name. She still can't, but she sits up there on her haunches, making out she's doing shorthand.

FOURTH WORKER Yes, he's had five different ones since I've been here.

ROSE Every time he opens his mouth Doris thinks it's the sermon on the mount.

DORIS Rose, duck, just 'cause your Keith's lost the scholarship I hope you ain't goin' to turn nasty with me. If you do, it don't make a scrap of difference to me . . . I like to be friendly. I'm always found all the gals here ever so nice to talk to, but if you want to spit your spite about you've picked on the right one with me. . . .

The Muddimans' kitchen

Gerry and Doris are in the kitchen, preparing to go to dinner with the Walshes. Paul is upstairs. Gerry is sitting at the table in his best suit. Doris is rushing in and out; she is turbulent and anxious, in contrast with Gerry's phlegmatic stillness.

DORIS   Gerry, there's sommat scruffy about you, even in the best suit money can buy. (*She picks bits of cotton from his clothes.*) Here, have a look at these earrings, are they tight, don't want them dropping down no grating. . . . Gerry, them nails are disgusting. Funeral nails our Mam used to call them. Go and clean 'em out if you're coming out with me.

GERRY   It's only Fontaine's dirt.

DORIS   Gerry, don't show them your awkward sides for God's sake. Try and behave like a decent human being, not like the wild man of Borneo, if you don't mind.

GERRY   Can't guarantee I won't blow orf once or twice during the course of the evening. Specially if the grub's a bit on the fancy side.

DORIS   Don't joke about it, it's too damn serious for that. And don't gollop your food down you the minute it's put in front of you. A leisurely dinner in the evening, it ain't the feed that counts. It's all the social give and take that matters . . . you can let me do the talking. (*Brushing her costume.*) Damn black, shows up all the bits. Smart though, you can't beat it. . . .

GERRY   Couple of stiff whiskies, Doris, I shall be kalied. I might give Madeleine's bum a tweak if there's anything to get hold of.

GERRY   Goo and clean your nails Gerry, don't spoil the ship for hap'orth of tar. . . . (*She shouts upstairs.*) Paul, come down here. . . . Let's have a look at you.
Intercut to Paul. He is upstairs in the bathroom making himself look handsome, and striking attitudes in front of the glass. He is rehearsing glittering dialogues that will never take place.

PAUL   (*into looking glass*) Why don't we go abroad, Madeleine . . . even if it only lasts a few months? I promise you, we'll neither of us ever regret it . . . we'll pack a lifetime's experience into a few short months . . . like Baudelaire. . . .
His reverie is interrupted.

DORIS   (*voice calling*) Are you all clean and sweet, Paul? Come on, let's have you down here. I've got sommat for you . . . (*Paul takes his*

68

leave of Madeleine for ever. "Adieu, fair lady", *and clatters down stairs.*)

GERRY Pooh, you make me sorry I ever ditched me bloody gas-mask.

DORIS You look lovely, Paul. You could be on the Rolf Harris Show with your figure.

GERRY He's on the Doris Muddiman Show already.

DORIS (*goes to the drawer. Takes object out of tissue paper.*) Here, I'm got summat special for you . . . I bin keeping it till you was really grown up and could appreciate it. It's your Grandad's gold hunter, it'll hang lovely on that three-piece suit . . . come here. . . .

PAUL Is it real gold?

DORIS Yes, and it keeps perfect time . . . (*She festoons him with the watch chain.*) You loop it across. (*She ranges it.*) Solid gold.

PAUL What's this, Mum?

DORIS That's what you call the fob. It's a bullet. He had it gold plated when they took it out of his belly when he was wounded on the Somme. It should've killed him by rights . . . it makes a lovely decoration. Gold suits you, Paul. . . .

The Walshs' patio

Dinner at the Ranch House, in celebration of the scholarship award to Paul. Madeleine and Robert, Doris and Gerry and Paul are there. Madeleine enters, leading them into the dining room.

MADELEINE I've put Paul next to me and Robert, you can come between Mr and Mrs Muddiman. All sit down.

ROBERT (*sociable, dreaming*) This is the way I like to see things run—the two sides of industry sitting down with good food between us instead of sheaves of paper. Friendly chat instead of acrimonious bargaining.

GERRY I like to know which side I'm on meself.

DORIS We're all on the same side, the side of business and progress. Isn't that right Mrs Walsh?

MADELEINE I personally wouldn't equate business with progress, but I'm rather eccentric in my opinions.

DORIS Oh. Isn't your cutlery heavy? I should've had a set like this coming to me. (*Nonplussed silence.*) Through a will. But I was done out of 'em by our Grace.
There is still a nonplussed silence.

PAUL They don't want to hear our murky family history, Mum.

MADELEINE Oh, is it murky? Do tell.

DORIS Paul, don't tell such lies. He's always romancing, Mrs Walsh.

ROBERT It would have to be very murky indeed to rival ours. Madeleine

69

has an aunt who's gone quite dotty, and thinks she's Catherine the Great.

Doris laughs dutifully.

GERRY (*heavily*) Do you know what Catherine the Great used to do? She had a specially picked guards regiment, that she collected together from all over Europe, and she kept them for her own pleasures. They all used to do that though, these big monarchs, before they was toppled.

There is a silence.

ROBERT It was a pretty close-run thing you know Paul. It was wide open till the last minute. I thought at one point the committee was seriously considering the Garfield boy, but he wanted to read Anthropology, and I think that's what did the trick for you.

DORIS (*indignant: falling into her natural way of speaking.*) I know for a fact Ede Garfield's up to her eyes in debt. She dunno which way to turn, does she Gerry? If the money had gone into her purse, it would a-gone on Bingo before it wenn on education . . . her, her. . . . (*Checking herself.*)

GERRY I don't think these things should be decided by committee, I think it should be merit alone. Smacks too much of the old boy network, dunnit?

ROBERT (*provoked*) Well Good God, that's the committee's job, to make the award according to merit. And I happen to think they've done it rather well. It sounds as if you had no very high opinion of your son's abilities.

DORIS He's pleased as punch really, same as I am. Paul's always been a real scholar, ever since he was no age at all.

MADELEINE (*graciously*) Well it was a pleasure to teach him French. And I don't think it was too tedious for him. Was it, Paul?

PAUL Yes . . . no . . . I mean . . . I couldn't have got an A pass without you.

DORIS Oo, we were ever so pleased with his French. He done better in that than he did in his own subjecks.

MADELEINE If I were in your place, Paul, I think I'd just throw everything in and go and study at the Sorbonne.

ROBERT Madeleine, don't be irresponsible. British industry needs scientists enough without you turning their heads with a lot of romantic nonsense. Besides, Fontaine is hardly going to hand out scholarships to young men to go and write graffiti all over the walls of Paris.

GERRY Well I think personally, there's too many young kids just growing up to be fodder for industry. Education should make you think for yourself.

70

DORIS (*trying to imitate Madeleine in gracious covering of awkward moment*) Gerry, you've dropped your serviette on the floor. You're treading on it . . . I'm always telling him about that at home.

ROBERT (*testily pursuing Gerry's point*) This disparagement of industry and business all the time, I really can't understand it. It's this country's lifeblood. It's not a second-best career, it's a damn fine one.

DORIS That's where the money is, and that's what most people want when all's said and done. And anybody who says different is a hypocrite. That's what I'm always telling Gerry, when he gets the hump over something that's upset him at Fontaine. I say "Yes, you don't get the hump when you open your pay packet".

MADELEINE Well at least I hope you won't drop French completely, Paul, if only for my sake. You can really read for pleasure now the exams are out of the way. Unless that's excluded under the terms of the scholarship. You can have any of my books.

DORIS That's very nice of you, Mrs Walsh. Paul, say "thank you". They all take it for granted you're going to do everything for them, don't they?

PAUL I want to get a lot of reading done this summer.

DORIS If you have time. I expect Fontaine'll want you to work there through the holidays, get to know the ins and outs of the firm. (*looks at Robert inquiringly*)

ROBERT Yes, I was hoping he would. We could use him. Put his French to some use. The girl who deals with out French correspondence has suddenly decided she's pregnant. At a very awkward moment for us. We're trying to get a foothold in French West Africa with a skin bleach. Seems to me extraordinary that the French firms don't do it, with their control of the market. But they don't. There's Chad, Dahomey and Mali—their governments have all been extremely responsive to our mission. . . .

DORIS Oooo, how interesting. You'll like that, Paul.

MADELEINE How repulsive. If I had the good fortune to be black, the last thing I'd want to do with my skin is start bleaching it.

GERRY I think it's a damn poor do, if you're reduced to making profit out of under-developed countries that are at starvation level.

DORIS Well you can bet your boots that all the money comes from us in the first place, in aid and that.

PAUL No, Mum, how can it? They were French countries, they belonged to the French.

DORIS Oh. Well then, if they don't belong to anybody now, they can do as they like with their money.

ROBERT (*patient condescension*) Now look here, let's try to be objective. It's surely a basic, human need to adorn oneself, to decorate oneself if you like. It's as basic and natural as eating, or sex itself. So that whenever I hear anyone say that the cosmetic industry is a fringe industry or immoral or something, I point out to them that it's one of the most basic facets of human nature.

GERRY Well it ain't in my nature for one. I wouldn't sell dye and chemicals that ain't worth the fancy packages they're wrapped in to anybody, whatever colour their skin is.

DORIS Get orf your soap-box for God's sake, Gerry.

GERRY Even if they've been brainwashed into thinking they want it. Their governments ought to step in and put a stop to it. It's wicked, it's a crime against humanity.

DORIS Eat your melon, Gerry, we're all waiting on you.

MADELEINE We shall never agree in a million years, so do let's stop it. It is Paul's day. Don't spoil it with political bickering.

ROBERT It's not bickering, it's an important issue. I can't understand why you work for Fontaine, feeling as you evidently do. If we're tainted by the money Fontaine brings into the country, then you are too. It's the same money.

GERRY To tell you the truth, I hate your bloody firm and all it stands for, and so do most of your workers in their heart of hearts.
There is a heavy silence.

DORIS Oo, Christ. (*Pretence gone, despair.*) I knoo this was going to happen if you came. I told you not to come. (*Shrieks.*) You ain't fit to be let out among decent yuman beings. . . . You ain't made nothing of your life, but you ain't going to ruin mine and Paul's . . . (*She ends with demented gulps and sobs.*)

MADELEINE Shall I bother to serve the next course?

GERRY No thanks, duck, I've had enough. Paul, you're old enough to do as you like. . . .

ROBERT They're incapable of rational argument without getting emotionally involved and resorting to personal abuse.

GERRY Doris, you can stay here if you like. But if you do, it's for good.

DORIS (*dithering*) Oo, I'm ever so sorry, Mr Walsh, he's always been like this . . . he makes me mouth and rave. It never was my disposition before I met him . . . Paul . . . you stay here and be nice to Mr and Mrs Walsh . . . tell 'em it ain't my fault . . . I'll make it up to you Mr Walsh, I've always bin ever such a good worker . . . there's nobody in the Hall of Perfumes puts in the hours I do . . . (*Hysterical.*) Ede Garfield don't pull her weight on that assembly line . . . she's a passenger, always has been . . . I'm bin ever so happy at Fontaine . . . don't let nothing happen just 'cause of him. . . .

Gerry pushes her before him towards the door. He turns for a last remark at the door.

GERRY All this hand in glove with management, it ain't right. If you want to know what they really think of you, ask 'em if they use the same shithouses in the factory. . . .

DORIS *(wildly)* Get out, get out, you're shown 'em how low bred y'are, get out for Christ's sake before they fetch the police.

They go. There is a frigid silence. Paul sits with his head in his hands. Robert and Madeleine exchange a glance.

ROBERT I'm hungry if you don't mind, Madeleine.

The Muddimans' kitchen

Doris and Gerry have just arrived home. There is a long tense silence. Doris moves about the kitchen, noisily and tragically, as though taking anticipatory leave of all her possessions. Gerry takes off his tie, opens his collar. He kicks off his shoes and lights a cigarette. Doris tidies up after him, ostentatiously dutiful.

GERRY *(provocatively)* Ain't enjoyed meself so much for a long time. Good night's work I reckon I done there. Pity you had to spoil it though, Doris, me duck. Y'expect your wife to back you up; that's what a wife's for.

DORIS *(hysterical rage)* Back you up? I'd bloody back you up, back you up agen that wall there and shoot yer. You'd better be on that doorstep when the Labour Exchange opens Monday morning . . . if they ain't already circulated your name all round the town.

GERRY I've only said what everybody else has been thinking. *(Grins.)* One bit of sauce they never thought they was going to get dished up with for dinner.

DORIS You've lost this house thirty-five quid a week clear, and there you sit looking as if you'd only got to sell your snot for silver florins. We're on the breadline from now on. Sell that damn car tomorrow, and I'll goo down the rag and bone shop with all me clothes . . . kiss the bloody Costa Brava goodbye, cost o' livin's all we'll have to worry about from now on. . . .

GERRY *(unmoved)* I thought to meself, I'm sick and tired of seeing the working people sing small in front of damned employers who give out work as if it were charity.

DORIS *(gusty sobs)* And Paul, how can he goo to college now? How can he goo to college with his parents on the dole, 'cause that's where we'll be, whether or no . . . that scholarship, it'll goo

73

straight to Rose's Keith now, land in his lap. You've made a gift of it to me worst enemy. (*Quietly.*) You must hate me, Gerry, to lay waste my life like you're done. Still, I know why you're done it, no matter what you say. Blart about principle, but it's revenge. Revenge, Spite. Revenge against me. 'Cause of Paul. 'Cause I'm closer to Paul'n what you are.

GERRY   I wouldn't want to be close to him. You're taught him to be a snob and a grabber. I'll tell you one thing, he's closer to the Walshes than he is to either of us. They can adopt him if they like. They have already. She has anyway.

DORIS   You can't see a scrap of good in anybody. You've always got to twist things round. Whether it's Fontaine, whether it's the Walshes, it don't matter who it is.

GERRY   The way she was flaunting herself in front of that boy, it made my heart heave.

DORIS   You'll be round there first thing in the morning with an apology. I ain't giving up everything I'm strived for. I ain't going to have it, it won't happen. Look at it, just look at it, what you've robbed me of. Hundred and fifty a year for that scholarship, me commission on Campaign thirty-nine—I was top of the averages in Zone 345, I'd got the gold medal bagged up . . . why didn't you put a knife in me ribs and have done with it? Not to mention our pensions, all we've paid in to that scheme. You'll never screw a penny of that back out them. . . .

GERRY   Money, you're that money mad, you jangle like a money box every time you open your mouth.

DORIS   You've helped dig me grave, Gerry, did that occur to you?

GERRY   Stop raving, Doris.

DORIS   I won't be here to rave much longer. I've got a cyst, big as that. (*She brandishes her fist, and thumps her bosom.*) There . . . I'm booked to goo in hospital in a fortnight, you never thought of that . . . I shouldn't survive the public wards, not now. I were going to have a private room through the Fontaine Scheme. I shall goo to the bottom of the waiting list for the Infirmary. It'll mean waiting two years, by which time I'll be lucky if I ain't dead of cancer. Then you can add murder to your list of crimes.

GERRY   'S only a cyst, Doris.

DORIS   Oh is it? That's what you think. You don't know what I'm bin through just lately. I ain't known where to put meself with it. Days I'm bin in agony sitting on that bench there.

GERRY   Well you won't have to sit there any longer. We'll live on my wage, like we used to.

74

DORIS Yis, I should like. Tell you one thing, it's only two incomes coming into this house that's kept me here. You're got two chances. You can goo round there and make it right with them, or you and me'll part company for good, sure as I stand here.

GERRY (*conciliating*) Don't get worked up, Doris, specially if you ain't well.

DORIS Worked up. I should think I've got a right to get worked up. Biggest wonder out I ain't gone off me bloody head with it, to see all I'm strived for knocked down and dragged through the mire. It's heartbreaking Gerry. (*Sobs.*) I shall crack up under this load; it's more than a sick woman can bear.

GERRY There ain't going to be no sacking, Doris. They don't sack you over things like that. I'm too good a workman, Doris . . . I was only talking for meself, Doris. It won't affect your position . . .

DORIS 'Course it affects my position. Everything you do affects my position. It's a family firm. (*Quoting.*) "For husband with wife, Fontaine has the good life." That's their policy. Look what happened to Kath Newberry, when they gave her the sack. She wenn and poured all that bleach over their flowerbeds. An hour later her husband had got his cards, and he hadn't done nothing. Gerry, you goo back up ther and apologise while there's still time.

GERRY You don't apologise for telling the truth, Doris. I don't goo on me belly to nobody.

DORIS All right, Gerry, that's the final curtain far as you and me are concerned. I don't reckon Paul'll want to stay here without me. I'm getting the bus to Peterborough first thing in the morning. It's bin a long line of humiliations the last few years. I can't swaller no more. You can go and throw your rubbish where you throw your love. But before I goo I shall ring up the bank, freeze the joint account. Then I'll have to goo and see a solicitor. I know where to find one: all them offices down the Parade with the gold writing on the winders, they're all solicitors and legal people. I'll let 'em know I'm separated from you, then they'll give me me job back. I'll disown yer, even if I have to put an advert in the local *Echo*.

GERRY Doris, you know what a big mouth I'm got. There's sommat in me makes me always got to say me piece, specially when I see injustice. It's for your sake, Doris, really. It sticks in me gills to see you and Paul surrendering yourselves body and soul to the ever open jaws of Fontaine. I'm always said, Doris, since the war the working people have thrown off their chains of iron and spun

THE PRESSURES OF LIFE

themselves chains of silk. But they're still chains, Doris, they
don't stop being chains. Can't you see, Doris, they've got you
where they want you now. You've got to show them you've still
got your independence and your pride.

DORIS   Gerry, if you don't stop talking twaddle I won't even stop here
till the first bus. I'll tramp the bloody streets tonight.

GERRY   I'll get a good job for both of us, Doris. I'll make amends if I've
done you any injury.

DORIS   There's only one way to make amends. I've told you what it is.

GERRY   I'll do anything for you, Doris, but I couldn't apologise to them.
I couldn't get the words out.

DORIS   You'll have to force them out, won't you? Paul's your trump
card, 'cause you know she likes him.

GERRY   You're harder than I'd ever know how to be Doris. I might say
me piece, but I ain't capable of cold-blooded calculations like
that.

DORIS   If you're too proud to go and say you're sorry for acting like a
pig, then I'm damn sure I'm too proud to stay under the same
roof with you a minute longer.

GERRY   I'll do anything you ask, Doris—

DORIS   I don't want anything else from you.

GERRY   Doris it ain't fair on me, it ain't fair.

DORIS   Ain't it?

GERRY   I'll tell you what, Doris, I'll write a letter. They'll get it first post
Monday morning.

DORIS   That ain't good enough.

GERRY   Doooriiis . . .

DORIS   Don't you "Doris" me. You goo round there and I might have
a bit of supper ready for you when you get back.
There is a long silence. She gets her suitcase down.

GERRY   I'll go and fetch Paul.

DORIS   (*triumphantly*) That's more like it. First bit of sense I've heard
from you tonight.
He goes. She starts preparing supper, singing to herself.

Walsh's office

*Opulent frond-filled office at the Production Centre. Personnel is in con-
ference with Robert Walsh and the Company Secretary.*
They are amid a welter of lists, charts etc.

COMPANY   Gentlemen, you know the position, I'm sure you're familiar
SECRETARY   with the instructions we've sent from H.Q. We have to effectu-
ate a rationalisation of labour which will involve the disposal

of ten per cent of the labour force in this plant.

PERSONNEL MANAGER (*nervous*) Er, it would be a pity for us to be compelled to initiate a programme of large-scale dismissals. Personnel has been assiduous in promoting a real sense of security among the staff. For us to start wholesale sackings now would be disastrous.

COMPANY SECRETARY Gentlemen, the word "fire" does not exist in the Fontaine vocabulary, except for the grossest industrial misconduct, sabotage and that kind of thing. The key word is redeployment. We found in Seattle that personnel who became superfluous are, quite frankly, an embarrassment to the company. So, in a way, we get them to fire themselves.

ROBERT But that seems most irregular according to British tradition. I'm afraid I'm puzzled. If you redeploy superfluous personnel, they don't become any less superfluous.

COMPANY SECRETARY Even in Fontaine there are certain jobs that are, to be frank, less pleasant than others. We found in Seattle that there were three areas where personnel was over-abundant. Quality control—Fontaine goods are invariably perfect if proper supervision is exercised at production level—creative marketing strategy, and zone data analysis. If we redeployed people from these departments to new jobs, which are alien to their intelligence and skills, they left of their own accord. Our research shows that a period of only three and a half weeks elapsed between our transfer and the voluntary submission of their resignation. In Seattle, we have the enviable record of having fired only seven individuals since nineteen hundred and fifty-nine.

PERSONNEL MANAGER (*approbatory murmur*) It would certainly relieve my department of a lot of headaches.

COMPANY SECRETARY From the statistical information I have here, you could take a long hard look at your own quality control. Some of these people aren't technicians at all. They have no formal, educational qualifications. Fontaine, with the best will in the world, simply cannot afford to go on carrying these people. In Seattle, we refer to them as lead souls.

ROBERT (*compliant*) It's rather convenient. Quality control has been precisely the area where the Fontaine spirit has had the least impact. There are one or two hot-heads it would give me the greatest pleasure to demote . . .

COMPANY SECRETARY Not to demote, Mr . . . Walsh. Redeployment. Now if you gentlemen can get to work on a couple of hundred names throughout this plant and submit them to me by tomorrow . . .

77

The Muddimans' kitchen

Gerry is sitting at home, dejected and immobile. It is late evening. Doris comes in, with her usual bustle and noise.

DORIS Oo, my God, what the hell are you playing at, sitting here in the dark? Frit me to death. Here's me, working the twilight shift, and all you can do is sit here twiddling your thumbs . . . you haven't so much as raised your hand to get me a bit of dinner . . . (*She becomes aware that something is wrong.*) What's happened? They've gev you the sack?

GERRY (*attempt at jauntiness*) That's more than they dare do.

DORIS Thank Christ for that. What they done then, made you Managing Director?

GERRY (*righteous*) Managing Director! I wouldn't take one of them parasite's jobs, even if they offered it . . . I'm bin . . . redeployed.

DORIS Oh, yes, where they put you? You know what that means don't you? You're on the way out.

GERRY I'm got a damn sight easier job. I shan't be breakin' me balls humping great sacks of chalk about.

DORIS Where they put you?

GERRY Dispatch . . . I shall be all right, only a few old codgers there too far over the hill to know what they're doin. . . . Wunn I have some fun, sending off all that garbage to the wrong places! I'll send hundreds of crates of Fandango Lotion to Outer Mongolia, sweeten up their yaks a bit. . . .

DORIS (*shrieks*) Sabotage, you can do time for that, Gerry . . . you're queered my pitch enough with that firm . . . so much silly bloody talk, you're mental. It's time you grew up, Gerry. Live in the real world. For God's sake, stop fighting yesterday's battles. All these years in your working life and you're ended up packing crates . . . what a yumiliation for me! You know who they put in there—all the peg-legs and the dibby buggers thay can't trust anywhere else . . . and they pay em rock bottom wages . . . what's your basic gooin to be?

GERRY I shall clear twenty.

DORIS Twenty quid. I shan't know where to put meself . . . ain't it all right eh? I thought the wife was only s'posed to goo out to work for pin money, and here's me finished up the bloody bread-winner . . . you're a proper Mary Anne, Gerry.

GERRY A man's gotter stick to his principles, Doris, even if it means a few bob a week less. It ain't nothing, Doris, compared to the struggles men and women of this country have had, to get the meagre rewards you take for granted today.

DORIS Principles, my Aunt Fanny. Your first principle should be to your family, same as everybody else's is . . . and judged by that you're a bloody poor specimen.

GERRY I don't have to go into Dispatch. I could leave. I could tell em what to do with their job . . . I'd get a job anywhere. If I stay on, it'll be because I want to, for me own ends. You can do more harm to an organisation working from the inside . . . I shall be a one-man fifth column . . . (*Mournful.*) I had this interview. Personnel. How they get these jobs I shall never know, talk about wheels within wheels—any road, he says "You're going to be redeployed." I thought to meself "Yis, and I'll do a bit of redeploying meself. I'll redeploy a few spanners in your works" . . . I'll start a union. Make a test case of it . . . I know a lot of blokes who'd be only too willing to join, given a bit of leadership.

DORIS Leadership, you. You can't even lead your own life.

GERRY Bit o' solidarity. They couldn't have mass sackings. They'd never get the labour.

DORIS Union, Blab-chops Union, that's all you're fit for. . . . Damn unions, goin' on strike over the least little thing. I'd strike if I had my way; I'd strike the buggers with red hot pokers . . . you want to thank your stars you're still got some work to go to, even if it is only a half-wit's. . . . Stop your rabble-rousing and do sommat useful. Put the kettle on . . . if you can't earn a man's wage, you can start doin' the bloody housework . . . (*She gabbles away.*)

The packing department

Gerry is at work in the packing department, a small room filled with boxes. He is involved in a menial job, with an old man, who is probably a pensioner doing part-time work. Gerry is packing and carrying cosmetics, and checking them off on a docket.

GERRY Twelve gross of Sno-Queen skin whitener—Republic of Dahomey. Four dozen Flagons Hint of Hibiscus—Turks and Caicos Islands. Four dozen carts of Rosebud Soaps to Laurence Marques. Who the bloody hell's Laurence Marques? . . . Angola . . . (*He sits down on the bench, talks to the old man.*) It's all right for you Dad, you only do it for pin money . . . (*Ruminative.*) Still . . . it's a living. . . .

The boardroom in America

The Economist, Chairman, Sociologist, and others, as at the start of the play.

CHAIRMAN   Gentlemen, the news is not good. Not good at all. We've had ten fat years, but it looks like the party is fini. . . . The European subsidiaries of Fontaine are being ruthlessly savaged by phenomenal labour costs, or what I call simple ole-fashioned greed. . . .

ECONOMIST   In UK we've reduced labour costs by one half, in France by one third . . . we can't do more than that. Fancy packaging needs the human touch.

     . . . Throughout British Industry there is an unfortunate tradition of obduracy and non-cooperation, non-union corporations feel the spin-off in absenteeism, malingering and sloppily-executed campaigns.

SOCIOLOGIST   The British still think the world owes them a living. The whole country seems to be reeling under a post-imperial malaise—

CHAIRMAN   I don't wanner hear about any malaise . . . I got too much of my own malaise. . . . Far as Fontaine is concerned, the UK is an economic dustbowl . . . let 'em have their high-wage economy, Fontaine's ain't footing the bill.

ECONOMIST   Does this mean we pull out fast?

CHAIRMAN   Fast? Fast as a tramp taking a welfare handout.

ECONOMIST   Yeh. But what happens to the plant, you can't just write it off?

CHAIRMAN   What plant? I got more plant in my solarium . . . and as for the production centre, some government bureau over there will always take it off our hands. . . .

SOCIOLOGIST   It's gonna make a ghost town of Litchborough.

CHAIRMAN   Ghost? Zombies! So what's gonna be the difference . . ? That's off the record, all that last bit. It's your job to prepare a statement . . . leak it to the local noos office . . . you know Fontaine regrets . . . a fruitful association . . . no longer reciprocally profitable . . . few jobs in Seattle for middle management and selected plant workers . . . skeleton distribution staff . . . generous severance pay . . . minimum of hardship et cetera et cetera. . . . Now gentlemen, this little setback is not going to affect Fontaine's expansion . . . but Europe has to learn that it's pricing itself way out of the market for investment in consumer luxuries . . . we gotta travel.

ECONOMIST   We gotta follow cheap labour. They may not be skilled but they'll work till they drop.

CHAIRMAN   Yeh, but don't try and sell me Asia, I'm not having my executives dying of yellerjack and plague. . . .

SOCIOLOGIST   What about a Muslim country? The women are getting more and more emancipated in the centres of sophistication and the tourist towns. When they throw off the veil there's gonna be an awful lot of pretty little dusky faces crying out for powder and

80

paint. And Fontaine has a duty to be there to supply the need.

CHAIRMAN (*ruminative, then enthusiastic*) Yeh. I like that. Fontaine will become an agent in the emancipation of women from their age-old servitude. We shall be a force for progress and enlightenment.

ECONOMIST Morocco and Tunisia are the really safe countries for foreign investors.

CHAIRMAN Morocco, did you say Morocco? I was in Morocco. Just three years back. They got a lot of freedom there, and some pretty plush hotels. . . .

ECONOMIST It's good for distribution, good for labour. Cost money for refrigeration but that'll be amply offset by profit margins from 23 per cent in UK to—at a rough computation to 67 to 70 per cent over the first ten years . . . there's a lot of centres, Fez, Marrakesh, Rabat. . . .

CHAIRMAN Fez? My wife fell in love with Fez. . . . (*Intercom.*) Get me two tickets executive class to Fez, Morocco . . . tomorrow or Friday. . . .

Speech Day
by Barry Hines

The Cast

Mr Warboys
Mrs Warboys
Danny, *their elder son*
Ronnie, *their younger son*
Mr Howard, *the Headmaster*
Mr Clarkson, *Deputy Headmaster*
Mr Douglas, *Senior Master*
Miss Bedford, *English teacher*
Mr Worrall, *Art teacher*
Mr Sanderson, *another teacher*
A Domestic Science Teacher
A Maths Teacher
Mr Rees, *Woodwork teacher*
A PE master
George, *the school handyman*
The Mayor
Professor Jessup
Grandpa
John ⎫
Martin ⎪
Robson ⎬ *boys of the school*
Wally ⎭
Julie
Shirley

Speech Day

The Warboys' kitchen

MR WARBOYS *We open with a group shot of the Warboys family around the table.*
The only things I can remember about history at school were, at the beginning of every lesson the history teacher used to say, "Right boys we'll pick up the threads from the last lesson". And once when we were doing Cromwell, I think it was before the battle of Naseby, when one of his officers told him that some of the men wanted to pray. "Let them pray if they like," he said "but tell them to keep their powder dry".

Cut to a close-up of Ronnie, and superimpose the title of the play over it.
Cut to a shot of the exterior of the flat by night. We can hear the National Anthem in the background.

Cut to a medium shot of Mrs Warboys in the Warboys' sitting room at the ironing board. The television is playing the National Anthem. She pauses to look off right to the TV, brushes blazer; puts it on a hanger. The camera pans her left to hang it below a shirt on the door.

The National Anthem ends. The camera pans her right to switch off the television set. She pauses a moment at the window, then she turns away.

Exterior early morning

Cut to a very long shot, high angle, over early morning town; zooming back through window frame.

We hear the sounds of milk bottles, and see a milk trolley on the balcony The milkman is delivering milk.

Cut to an inside shot of the parents' bedroom. Mr Warboys reaches out to stop alarm. He gets out of bed, comes to the camera, calling to Danny.

MR WARBOYS Come on Danny—let's be havin' yer. . . . (*knocking on door*) Danny—come on Danny—let's be 'aving yer.
Inside Danny's bedroom, we see him start getting up.

Exterior factory

Close group shot of men arriving at work. We see Mr Warboys go by in close-up. Then we see Danny clocking in.

Interior factory/Danny starting work

Cut to

Interior boys' bedroom
A medium shot of Ronnie still asleep.
Cut to

Exterior flats
A long shot of Ronnie on his way to school.

Interior factory
We see a steel furnace. A truck is coming from furnace pulling out and moving away.
Close-up of a man drinking tea with Mr Warboys who is reading a paper.

MR WARBOYS What about this two pound limit on rises then, Joe?
Cut to a long shot of the school buildings. We hear the Headmaster's voice. Then we move into the school hall, and see him on the platform.

HEADMASTER The timetable will be as normal this morning. Will all pupils who are receiving prizes this afternoon meet in the hall for a short while directly after break this morning. The Speech Day Ceremony will commence at two o'clock. Stay in your own form rooms after the afternoon registration and each form will be sent for individually.

Outside the school
Miss Bedford is just getting out of her car and closing the door. She turns as Ronnie comes up.

MISS BEDFORD Good morning, Ronnie.

RONNIE Late again, Miss.

MISS BEDFORD You can talk, lad.

RONNIE Five minutes late. You'd have time stopped at our Danny's place for that.

MISS BEDFORD Time stopped?

RONNIE Yeh. They allow 'em three minutes a week. Anything over that they knock 'em half an hour's pay off.

The factory
We see Danny and an old man finishing drinking tea, throwing away the paper cups and going off.

The school hall
HEADMASTER I do not have to tell you, of course, that important guests will be in school this afternoon. You will be under public scrutiny. Your conduct will be impeccable, your appearance immaculate, which means, of course, full school uniform. That is all. Dismiss.
We see the pupils beginning to leave and the Headmaster watching them.

Outside the hall

The Headmaster comes out, down the steps to look around. He sees some litter and goes back in.

In the classroom Ronnie, Wally, and other boys are seen playing "Hands".

The Headmaster walks along the corridor to a notice board on the wall. He runs his finger along the board.

The Headmaster's study

The Headmaster is looking out of the window, talking to Mr Clarkson.

HEADMASTER   I'm a little concerned about the school grounds, Mr Clarkson. I thought it might look a shade tidier.

MR CLARKSON   Do you want me to ask George to see to it?

A classroom

Ronnie and the others are settling down. Miss Bedford is handing out books.

MISS BEDFORD   Right, boys, I'm going to give you a treat today.

The boys start to laugh and hum "The Stripper," miming the actions.

The Headmaster's study

HEADMASTER   Could you please see to those arrangements, Mr Clarkson?

MR CLARKSON   Would you mind if I asked Mr Douglas to attend to it Headmaster? I really am up to the neck, what with one thing and another.

HEADMASTER   Certainly. Let's have all the senior staff pulling their weight. After all, that's what we're paid extra for.

The classroom

MISS BEDFORD   Soccer and sex, that's all you think about.

WALLY   We never said a word, Miss.

MISS BEDFORD   You didn't have to, did you? Now look after these books, lads. They've just arrived and you're the first class in the school to use them. In my opinion this is one of the best sets of stories around today.

JOHN   The best books for the best class, eh Miss?

MISS BEDFORD   That's right, John. (*She sits on the desk and opens the book.*) Now I'll just tell you something about the author before we begin. (*She notices a boy yawning.*) Come on, Martin, now don't say you're bored. We haven't even started yet.

MARTIN   I'm not, Miss. I'm just tired that's all.

JOHN   There's no wonder. He's out with his bird every night.

87

MARTIN Am I, heck!

JOHN You are. I see you come past our house.

MARTIN Like to bet?

JOHN Well nearly every night, then.

MARTIN Well, for thy information, I only see her four or five nights a week.

ROBSON Why don't you get married to her then?

As the class and Miss Bedford are laughing, enter Mr Douglas, the Senior Master. The attitude of the boys changes. They rise.

WALLY Here comes . . . Dracula.

Mr Douglas stands in the doorway to dramatise the effect.

MR DOUGLAS All right. You can sit down and keep quiet.

(*He closes the door and crosses the room. Miss Bedford joins him.*) Miss Bedford. I'm afraid I've got a bit of bad news for you, Helen.

MISS BEDFORD Yes?

MR DOUGLAS The boss wants these lads to help George in the garden. So you'll have to have the rest of the period off. (*Miss Bedford smiles briefly. He had expected her to beam with relief.*) You don't mind, do you?

MISS BEDFORD No, I don't mind.

MR DOUGLAS (*to the class slowly*) Right, lads, I've got a job for you. I want you to report round to George at the Greenhouse. There's some jobs want doing for this afternoon. All right. Off you go!

The boys rise and go out, leaving the books on the desk. Mr Douglas follows them out, closing the door. Miss Bedford starts gathering up the books.

The school greenhouse

George, the school handyman, is waiting for the boys, who are just coming towards him.

RONNIE We've come to help you, George.

GEORGE Of course you've come to help me. You didn't expect them to send 5A down to help me, did you?

RONNIE What do you want us to do?

GEORGE I don't want you to do owt. There's nowt to do, and even if there was it's nothing to do with you gang anyway. But His Master's Voice thinks different, so we'd better go through the motions if we do nowt else.

The staff room

MR SANDERSON You're not usually free this lesson are you, Helen?

HELEN   No. I should be taking 5G1, but the girls are doing the eats for this afternoon, and the boys have just been taken away to help in the garden or something.

SANDERSON   That's a nice little bonus for you. Nobody ever takes them anywhere when I have them.

Outside the greenhouse

GEORGE   You lot, get those sacks and go round and see if you can find any waste paper. You lot, there's some forks and spades there. Have a go between the shrubs. Wally and Rob do a bit of weeding in that long border. There's some magnifying glasses and tweezers on the bench at the back of the door. (*The boys laugh, and go off.*) Ronnie, run over the lawns again will you? Not that you'll get owt off. But if he hears the noise of the engine that will keep him happy. Come on, lads, get moving. And mind you only do the front of the school. That's all that matters, lads.

The domestic science room

Ronnie is leaning in the window to Shirley.

RONNIE   Pass us a bun, Shirl.

SHIRLEY   I can't do that.

RONNIE   Course you can. They'll not miss one.

SHIRLEY   I'll get into trouble.

RONNIE   Who are you feeding anyway? Look at 'em all.

SHIRLEY   There's a lot of guests coming, you know. There's the Mayor and his wife and somebody from a University. There's the staff and all the prizewinners and their parents . . .

RONNIE   Never mind all them. Let me have one.

Shirley reaches for a cream cake and passes it to Ronnie, who goes off.

SC.TEACHER   What are you doing there, Shirley? Come on now, get on with those butterfly buns.

SHIRLEY   Miss, I'm just opening the window a bit wider. It's red hot in here.

The playground

A wide shot of boys picking up litter. We cut to another part of the grounds. Robson and another boy are on their knees weeding below some steps. We see a close-up of hands clenched. They open to drop two earwigs on the ground.

ROBSON   First one at edge is the winner. Right! On your marks. Get set. Go. . . .

A classroom

The noise of the lawn mower is heard. The Maths Teacher is at the board explaining.

MATHS TEACHER   And therefore A and C is equal to . . . and similar ADO is congruent to . . .

He is exasperated by the noise. Crosses to the window, opens it, and waves the ruler, calling to Ronnie.

MATHS TEACHER   Hey you, lad!

The class are enjoying the diversion. Ronnie leaves the mower running and comes to the window. He takes the ruler from the teacher.

RONNIE   It's not mine, sir.

He hands it back, but drops it.

MASTER   I know it's not yours, idiot. Pick it up. Pick it up. It's mine. I was using it to attract your attention as you appear to be stone deaf.

RONNIE   It's the engine, sir.

MASTER   Yes, I'm well aware of that. How do you expect people to work with that din going on outside?

RONNIE   It's not my fault, sir. It's Mr Howard who wants it doing.

MASTER   Well, can't you work somewhere else, and come back to this part later?

RONNIE   Mr Howard says it's got to be done now, sir.

MASTER   Well can't you use a handmower or something, then? It would be much quieter.

RONNIE   You what, sir? A handmower! It's bad enough running this thing up and down, without taking all morning about it.

MASTER   All right then. But be quick about it and come back to this part later.

The staff room

MISS BEDFORD   (*reading a report*) "Shirley must work harder . . . Shirley is easily distracted from her work . . . has made little effort this year. . . . Satisfactory. . . . Fair. . . . Shirley is not working to her full capacity. . . . Shirley could do better if only she tried harder. . . . " Of course she could do better, if only they gave her something better to do.

MR SANDERSON   Don't let it get you down, love. They'll be on their travels in three weeks' time.

MISS BEDFORD   Yes, but there'll be another lot to come back to in September, won't there?

The classroom

Ronnie is still outside talking through the window to the Maths Teacher.

90

RONNIE   You don't think I like doing this, do you?

THS TEACHER   Don't be cheeky, lad. What's your name?

RONNIE   Ronnie Warboys.

THS TEACHER   Right, Warboys. I'll have a hundred lines from you by to-morrow morning: "I must not be insolent to a member of the staff." Now get about your business, and get away from this part of the school as quickly as possible.

He slams the window. We see Ronnie going back to the mower, and turning to put his tongue out at the window.

(*who has returned to the board*) Right, come on now. Let's settle down. It's all right for him; he's nothing better to do with his time. I've got to get you lot through an examination at the end of next year.

The greenhouse

GEORGE   I suppose you've hired a Pickford's van for this afternoon, Ronnie?

RONNIE   What do you mean?

GEORGE   To take your prizes home in.

RONNIE   You must be joking. A Dinky van'd be too big for what I'm getting.

GEORGE   Any big-wigs coming?

RONNIE   I don't know. The Mayor's coming I think, and some bloke from a University.

GEORGE   Joe Brannigan! Is he coming?

RONNIE   Who the hell's Joe Brannigan?

GEORGE   The Mayor.

RONNIE   Do you know him or summat?

GEORGE   I should think so. We worked together at Leonard and Wolfe for fifteen years.

RONNIE   My dad works there. They're laying 'em off left right and centre just now though.

GEORGE   We started off in the moulding bay together. We were both shop stewards there.

RONNIE   My dad works in the melting shop. Our Danny's at Brightside Steel. I was thinking of going there, but our Danny says there's no chance. Did they make you redundant, George?

GEORGE   No, I got a hernia and then I did my back. The doctor said I'd be better off finding a lighter job.

RONNIE   Our Danny did his back at work. That's why he stopped playing football. He went for trials with United when he was at school, you know, our Danny.

The woodwork room

The boys are getting out their jobs at the start of a lesson.

RONNIE Making firewood again, Wally?

WALLY My dad brings better looking firewood than this from work.

Enter Mr Rees, the Woodwork Master.

MR REES Don't bother getting your jobs out, lads. We've got a job to do down the hall.

RONNIE What, sir?

MR REES We've got to get the chairs out for this afternoon.

RONNIE That's not right, sir.

A BOY It's always us. Why is it always us, sir?

ROBSON I'm not doing it.

A BOY I want to get on with my table. I'll never get it finished.

RONNIE Ay. We've done gardening an' all before break.

MR REES Don't blame me, lads. I'm just told what to do, the same as you are. Come on now. Leave your jobs out and we'll put them away later on. Aprons off, blazers on. Come on now. Quick as you can down to the Hall.

The stage in the school hall

MR REES Listen! I want six rows of chairs across this platform facing that way. Everybody do that except Rob, Wally, and Ronnie. You come with me. Come on, lads. Get on with it. (*They jump down from the stage and move into action.*)

MR REES (*holding a plan*) Right, lads. Now this is the plan. Behind the velvet curtains are the soft-bottomed chairs, Wally, for the VIP's. They're going to be sitting here, just here. Those with the arms . . . four behind this table.

George enters with a cactus, and places it on the table.

GEORGE That's good enough for them buggers who'll be at this table.

We see the boys at work; then cut to a table laid for tea, with waitress to one side. Finally we see Mr Clarkson, who is in charge of the prize-winners.

MR CLARKSON Now just be quiet for a minute, lads, while we go through this rehearsal. Right. I presume you're all here. (*He notices Ronnie's feet and raps on the table.*) Hey! Legs off that chair. (*Ronnie takes his legs down, and swings round.*) Now when your name is called, approach the platform smartly, climb the steps on the right, walk across the front of the platform to Professor Jessup, who will be standing here.

Medium close-up shot of boys at the other end of the hall, seated. The camera pans along their faces from left to right.

92

CLARKSON Shake hands, receive your prize, certificate, or whatever it may be in your hand, then walk across the stage, down the steps and back to your place. Got that? Right, let's have a quick run through. David Stacey, let's have you first, you should know the ropes. (*David comes up, and shakes hands.*) Well done. Good. (*Calling out.*) Margaret. (*She comes up to pretend to take her prize.*) Malcolm Priestley.

As he comes up to the platform, another boy comes into the hall, and approaches Mr Clarkson with a message.

BOY Excuse me, sir. Mr Howard wants to see you in his room.

CLARKSON Right. Thank you lad. (*To prizewinners.*) If you'll just wait here I'll be back as quickly as possible.

We see the chairs of boys who have now finished.

MR REES Right lads. Come on. That's it.

They jump down from the platform: the camera holds Robson who picks up the cactus and holds it out to the prizewinners.

ROBSON Shake hands with that then.

He replaces it. The prizewinners laugh. Robson jumps down, and catches up with the others.

MR REES That's great. It's nearly bell time. We'll have five minutes before it goes. (*To Ronnie.*) Are your parents coming this afternoon, Ronnie?

RONNIE What for? I haven't won owt.

MR REES You don't need to have won anything.

RONNIE There's no point in losing a shift for nowt is there?

MR REES What about your mother?

RONNIE She's working. She's got a job at Laidlaws.

MR REES You must be rollin' in it at your house then, your Mother, your Dad, and your Danny all working.

RONNIE You what? She's not bothered about working. But what with my dad in danger of being thrown off and our Danny's only on apprentice money, she thought she'd better get a job while there was one going, just in case. She doesn't like it though—doing seams all day—bores her to tears. Funny thing is she likes dressmaking an' all. But not doing the same thing over and over again. She says it drives her mad.

The bell rings. We cut to a corridor with pupils coming out of rooms; then to a canteen queue; and, finally, George taking plants into the Hall. Ronnie, Rob, and Wally are seen going out of school, kicking an old box around on a patch of waste ground, and then coming out of a fish-and-chip shop, with chips in paper.

RONNIE One, two, three, four! Scratch your eyes out, sweetie!

ROBSON   I say let's wag it and go for a game of snooker.

RONNIE   We could say we got food poisoning from these chips.

Top deck of a bus

RONNIE   Anyway, what do you want to wag it for, Rob, when you're getting a prize?

ROBSON   Am I?

RONNIE   You are. They've invented a new prize. The detention prize. For the most detentions in the history of the school.

ROBSON   Let's face it. I'd win that easy enough.

RONNIE   There ought to be prizes for things like that. Why do they always give prizes for lads with the biggest brains? Why not a prize for the lads with the biggest appetite?

ROBSON   Wally'd win that easy. All that stuff he eats, I don't know where he puts it all.

RONNIE   It goes straight down his legs into his boots.

WALLY   What about a prize for the biggest creep?

RONNIE   Stacey'd win that easy.

ROBSON   He's won it. He's getting a prize for special services to the school or summat like that.

RONNIE   What about old Rodgers?

ROBSON   The best dressed man in England.

WALLY   Seen his suit?

RONNIE   He's going to sell it to the British Museum.

ROBSON   I know, the mask prize for the best-looking bird.

RONNIE   Miss Crampton.

WALLY   She'd win easy. Seen her specs? They're just like jam jar bottoms.

RONNIE   It's be great wouldn't it? And why don't they have somebody like Racquel Welch or George Best, somebody like that instead of somebody we've never heard of? Who is it this afternoon, a professor from a university? Who wants to listen to him? I'd sooner listen to me old man any time.

ROBSON   They ought to have asked him, Ronnie.

RONNIE   They did but he couldn't make it. His Rolls broke down. Haven't you seen it jacked up outside our flat?

The school art exhibition

MR REES   (*looking at some object*) Who made it?

MR WORRALL   Charlie Bradford.

MR REES   Charlie Bradford! Would you believe it?

MR WORRALL   He were a good 'un, Charlie. When he were here.

MR REES   Didn't he want to take it home?

MR WORRALL   Can you imagine how long it would have lasted in their house? Anyway, they can't take them home. I mean what are all the inspectors, governors and mayors going to do if they all took them home?

MR REES   There's some good stuff here, Stan.
There's some great stuff.

MR REES   Do any of them follow it up after they've left school? I mean do they ever come to your art classes?

MR WORRALL   A few. For a year or two, then they drop off. When I was at college and regarded myself as Pablo's natural successor I once took a holiday job on a building site. When I got home at nights I didn't want to know about painting, I was too shagged out.

MR REES   (*looking at a painting of "Jarrow Crusade"*) Just look at that! That's terrific!

The staff room

Three teachers are chatting. Julie comes over for the cups.

JULIE   Excuse me, sir. Have you finished with your cup?

MR SANDERSON   Yes, you can take it, Julie. (*Julie stoops to pick up the cups.*) I thought you'd have been bringing a few cakes around with the tea, Julie. All this catering you've been doing this last couple of days. I thought there might have been one or two left over for the workers.

JULIE   What about us, sir?

MR SANDERSON   She'll make a lovely barmaid in a few years' time will Julie. I only hope she finishes up at my local.

We see some other teachers playing bridge as Julie takes the cups out.

School entrance

We see a bus pulling in, and a group of boys getting off. A car comes into the school, and sounds its horn for the boys to move. They leap to one side as it goes by. Ronnie is seen making a "V" sign. Parents and pupils are moving towards the school.

5G1's form room

MR SANDERSON   It's a good job you lot will be sitting at the back where nobody can see you. (*Pause.*) It's a pity they don't darken the auditorium during the performance like they do at the theatre. Clarke, I thought I told you to go home and change that shirt? It is Speech Day you are attending lad, an occasion of dignity and decorum. Not a rave-up in some gloomy smoke-filled cellar.

CLARKE   What's a rave-up, sir?

MR SANDERSON   A white shirt, lad. You heard what Mr Howard said.

CLARKE   I haven't got a white shirt, sir.

MR SANDERSON   Nonsense, lad. Everybody's got a white shirt.

CLARKE   I've got a white T-shirt with a Mickey Mouse on the front.

MR SANDERSON   Mickey Mouse on Speech Day! Good God! The end is surely imminent. (*Pause while he passes to Robson.*) Robson, you can't possibly go into the hall wearing that leather jacket. In fact you shouldn't be wearing it in school at all. You've been told often enough about it.

ROBSON   It's not only me. . . . I'm not the only one without school uniform on, sir.

MR SANDERSON   I am painfully aware of the fact that you are not all wearing school uniform, Robson, but the others are at least wearing decent jackets.

ROBSON   I'm wearing a jacket.

MR SANDERSON   Yes, I know, but there's a difference.

ROBSON   I know there is. Theirs is made out of animal hair, mine's made out of animal skin. That's the difference.

MR SANDERSON   Yes, but yours is not acceptable and there the matter rests. Why can't you people be sensible about these matters?

The school entrance

A car drives up to the main door. A medium shot of the Headmaster and Prefects at the top of the steps waiting.

We see groups of pupils watching for various visitors. The Mayor's car is at the steps. A chauffeur opens the door for the Mayor to get out. He helps the Lady Mayoress out, and they come forward.

George comes up with his wheelbarrow. Before they pass him, he drops it and speaks to them.

GEORGE   Now then Joe, how's it going then? Hello Edna, are you all right, love?

But they pass on, completely ignoring him. They go up the steps to be greeted by the Headmaster.

HEADMASTER   . . . Good afternoon . . . shall I lead the way?

They go in through the main doors.

5G1's form room

MR SANDERSON   It's a good job you're not going up on the stage wearing that skirt, Jean, or there'd be a few raised eyebrows. (*Ronnie whispers to Robson.*) That's enough of that, Warboys. And just look at the state of your shirt, lad.

96

RONNIE　I know, and it was clean on an' all this morning, sir.

MR SANDERSON　What've you been doing?

RONNIE　I've been gardening and shifting chairs all morning, that's what I've been doing. Don't know why we don't come to school in overalls—I don't know about white shirts.

They are interrupted by an announcement by Mr Clarkson over the public address system.

MR CLARKSON　Attention! Attention! This is the deputy Headmaster speaking. Would the rest of the 5th year, that is Forms G1, G2, G3, G4 now move along to the Hall, please. Thank you.

The school corridor

MR DOUGLAS　Move your feet not your tongues. Keep the noise down. Come here. Straighten your tie. Smarten yourselves up a bit. Come on. Stop there. Vicky. Why must you be different from everybody else? Are any of the other girls wearing pullovers? Take it off. Robson! Come here, lad. (*To others.*) Stop there. Were you in Assembly this morning?

ROBSON　Yes, sir.

MR DOUGLAS　Did you hear what the Headmaster said about wearing school uniform? Take it off. (*He takes jacket.*) Warboys! Straighten your tie. Do up your shirt. Pull down your sleeves. The rest of you carry on. Right. Off you go.

The staff room

Mr Clarkson enters.

MR CLARKSON　Could I have your attention please? The children are almost assembled, so if you could be ready in about five minutes. . . .

As he goes we see the teachers getting ready. Mr Rees comes to attention.

MR REES　Well it looks as if everybody's getting togged up, I suppose I'd better nip along to the Woodwork Shop. I think I've got a clean smock down there.

P.E. MASTER　Fetch my track suit will you, Dave, while you're at it.

MR REES　Eh, I wonder if the needlework department could sew us a bit of fur on the collars, so that we don't feel out of it?

We see the other teachers putting on their academic gowns.

P.E. MASTER　What about those rabbits they've got over in the biology lab?

MR REES　It all depends. What colour are they?

P.E. MASTER　They're old English. White with a black stripe and a few spots.

MR REES　Just the job. It'll go well with that khaki smock of mine, a bit of fur round the collar. Let's join the mob.

The school hall

The choir are sitting waiting. The hall is full of parents, and behind them the pupils. In one group we see a boy take a book from a pocket of a boy, who then hits another.

The Headmaster's study

HEADMASTER Is everything all right, Mr Mayor? Is there anything I can do for you?

MAYOR (*holding out sherry glass*) Aye. Is there any chance of changing this for a bitter?

HEADMASTER (*smiling*) Excuse me. (*He goes to the door.*) Excuse me, ladies and gentlemen. It appears that everything is ready and the school is waiting. So when you are ready we will make our way along to the Hall.

We see the group coming along the corridor, and then cut to a wide shot of the school hall, with prizes and cups on a table, and then to the parents. A close-up of Ronnie looking towards the parents.

We hear the dialogue flashback over the hall scene:

MRS WARBOYS It'll go down in history this you know, all sat down having an evening meal together.

Cut to:

The Warboys' kitchen

MR WARBOYS I'll bet that bugger who invented shifts never had to work them.

DANNY Does old McIntosh still take history, Ronnie?

RONNIE He don't take us. He only takes top forms.

DANNY I can remember one time when we used to drive 'im mad. We used to stick drawing pins in the ceiling before he came in and he could never understand how we did it.

Danny waits for one of them to ask how they did it.

RONNIE Go on then. Tell us if you're gonna.

DANNY We used to balance a drawing pin on top of a window pole, lift it up, then bang it into the ceiling. Old McIntosh could never understand how they'd got rammed in so hard.

MRS WARBOYS It's a pity you'd nowt else better to do. You didn't half waste your time at school, Danny.

MR WARBOYS He wouldn't have been ramming drawing pins into the roof if they'd have been doing the history of United.

RONNIE No.

MR WARBOYS If he'd sat on one he'd never have noticed, he'd have been that interested.

99

The school hall

The procession enters, and we cut from long shots of the visitors and governors to close-ups of Robson and Ronnie watching.

The procession scales the stage, and everyone takes their seats.

HEADMASTER We will begin our Speech Day by spending a few moments in silence, collecting our thoughts, and remembering what we are doing and why we are here.

Let us give thanks, O God, for this school, for our founders and governors. For our relatives and friends, and for all who in their generation have built up that which we inherit.

CHORUS Lord hear our prayer, and let our cry come unto thee.

HEADMASTER That thou wilt bless all members of this school, those who rule and those who obey, those who teach and those who learn, that, being not slothful in business but keen in spirit, we may with all diligence serve thee.

CHORUS Lord hear our prayer and let our cry come unto thee.

HEADMASTER Grant that we who receive rewards for our labours may always remember that such talents as we . . . (pardon me) . . . possess come from thee, and that from those to whom much is given— much will be expected.

Cut to a flashback:

Outside Grandpa's house

Two Jehovah's Witnesses backing away

GRANDPA (*shouting*) I'll give you spirit of God! What's God ever done for us? Just tell me that. You want to chuck them Bibles away and get your bloody history books out.

RONNIE You'll be badly again, Grandad.

GRANDPA Who's side's God on any road? that's what I'd like to know. Not ours I can tell you. He's got a terrible record as far as our side's concerned.

RONNIE Grandad, calm down. You'll be havin' another do.

GRANDPA (*still shouting*) It's some bloody work you want! Bloody Bible punchers.

The school hall

HEADMASTER* "I have a dream. The past decade has been a most exciting one. In spite of the tensions and uncertainties of our age something profoundly meaningful has begun. Old systems of exploitation and oppression are passing away and new systems of justice and equality are being born. In a real sense ours is a great time in which to be alive. Therefore I am not discouraged

100

about the future. Granted that the easy-going optimism of yesterday is impossible. Granted that we face a world crisis which often leaves us standing amidst the surging murmur of life's restless sea. But every crisis has both its dangers and its opportunities. Each can spell either salvation or doom. In a dark, confused world the spirit of God may yet reign supreme."

* He is reading from a famous speech by the American, Martin Luther King.

Cut to a flashback:

Top of bus

ROBSON They ought to have asked Wally to read instead.

WALLY Oh shut it, Rob. I can read if I want to.

ROBSON Ar, the Dandy and Beano.

WALLY I can read as good as you any day.

ROBSON You what? What about when we're reading round the class.

WALLY That's because I get nervous. I don't like reading like that.

RONNIE As though they'd ask Wally to read on Speech Day. He hasn't got a white shirt for a start, and look at his hair. They wouldn't let him near the stage with hair like that.

ROBSON Have thee heard 'im, Ronnie? He sounds just like Professor Stanley Unwin.

WALLY Do I heck?

ROBSON Go on then, show us.

WALLY All right then I will.

RONNIE Here, read this, Wally: "School-leavers' plight." That's us isn't it?

WALLY *(reading)* "Young people leaving school without qualifications tend to take several jobs in quick succession, until at seventeen they are among the long-term unemployed. The number of jobs for the less able appears to be getting fewer every year and many of these are in the manual category. . . ."

The school hall

HEADMASTER Last year seventeen former pupils of this school gained university degrees, including that of John Davis, who was the first pupil at this school to be accepted at Cambridge University. John was awarded the degree of B.A. with second class honours in geography and we are all very proud of his achievements.

Cut to a flashback:

The sports field

MR DOUGLAS Now then, Warboys. Where does this event appear on the programme?

RONNIE It's a new event, sir.

MR DOUGLAS It's a very old event, lad. And definitely an out-of-school activity. Off you go and get yourselves involved in a bit of legitimate athletics.

The school hall

HEADMASTER Last year our academic record achievement was the best to date. We had more "A" level, "O" level, and CSE successes than in any previous year . . .

WALLY What about Stuart Baraclough? He's only playing for Newcastle, that's all.

RONNIE He might not have got any "O" levels.

WALLY "O" levels! You mean he was in 5G like us.

HEADMASTER . . . something of which the school can be justly proud. And now breaking with tradition, which can be a healthy thing at times, the school choir will entertain us with two modern folk songs under the direction of Mr Hill.

CHOIR Now England is a democratic place.
The English are a tolerant race.
Any man may have his say.
But when it comes to Polling Day,
It's down with taxes up with pay,
And damn the poor!
Charity! Charity!
Dives was a charitable man.
We see the Headmaster and the Lord Mayor clapping, and pan along the other guests, all applauding.

HEADMASTER It now gives me great pleasure to introduce to you our guest of honour this afternoon, Professor Jessup, Vice-Chancellor of Gloucester University, who will now present the prizes and certificates, and later on in the programme give the address. Professor Jessup.
(*Applause.*)

ROBSON Bloody hell, I've had enough of this.

PROFESSOR Thank you very much. (*He starts the prize giving.*) Special prizes for services to the school: David Stacey and Margaret Shipman. (*Applause.*)

PROFESSOR The Leonard and Wolfe Essay Prize—Pauline Radcliffe.
Cut to a flashback:

102

The street

DANNY What about that 650, Ronnie?

RONNIE I'm going to get a bike as soon as I start work.

DANNY You're going to pay cash, aren't you, out of your first wage packet?

RONNIE I'll get one.

DANNY That's what I said.

RONNIE Well, why don't you then?

DANNY Because I can't afford it. I've no chance of paying cash.

RONNIE What d'you want to pay cash for . . .

DANNY And I daren't risk repayments just now with only six months of my apprenticeship to run.

RONNIE What do you mean? I thought you said you'd soon be getting top money.

DANNY Getting my cards more like. It's a right swindle. Take an apprenticeship they said at school. Don't go into a dead-end job. And what happens? You work for pocket money for five years and then you suddenly find that you're not even guaranteed a job at the end of it. "Owing to the fluctuating economic factors and the variable state of the Home and Foreign markets"—it's nowt but slave labour, that's what it is.

A wide shot of football fans coming towards camera, singing and clapping. Danny and Ronnie move forward and the oncoming group jostle past them.

The school hall

The choir are preparing to sing the second folk song.

CHOIR Oh what a piece of work is man.
How marvellously wrought;
The quick contrivance of his hand,
The wonder of his thought.

Why need we look for miracles,
Outside of nature's laws;
When man is what to wonder at
With every breath he draws.

But give him room to move and grow,
But give his spirits play
And he can make a world of light,
Out of the common clay.
Cut to a flashback:

Grandpa's house

RONNIE Hello, Grandad.

GRANDPA Now then, Ronnie. I wondered who it was. What you doing down here? Have you got lost?

RONNIE I just come to see how you were.

GRANDPA Don't try and soft-soap me you young bugger. What are you after now?

RONNIE I'm not after owt.

GRANDPA I've heard that before. What was it last time you came, that fishing basket of mine?

RONNIE Are you going to watch football after this, grandad?

GRANDPA I told you there was summat in it didn't I?

RONNIE Our tele's gone.

GRANDPA What do you mean? They've taken it back to the shop? That's the trouble with that hire purchase . . .

RONNIE No it's broke down. Me Mam was plugging in iron and television picture went off. My Dad says it must have fused or summat.

GRANDPA Tell me the old, old story. Do you know if it wasn't for the fact that I can't afford to have it mended I'd have put my stick through that screen many a time.

RONNIE Well hang about, Grandad, it'll be going off soon.

GRANDPA Things are going to change. It's going to be a better tomorrow. Bugger tomorrow; what about today? I might not be here tomorrow.

RONNIE Great. It's gone off. We might see summat on interesting now.

GRANDPA There's going to be change. Things are no better now than when I were a lad. There's still bad houses and bad hospitals and bad schools. There's still unemployment and the dole. And it's still the same folk telling us what to do.

RONNIE Who do you think will win, Grandad?

GRANDPA There might be a few bigger crumbs now and again. But I agree with what Lenin said, when he said we ain't interested in size of crumbs, or even slices of cake. We want bakery, he said, so that we can determine the sort of cake that's to be baked.

The school hall

MAYOR It's a bit different from when I was at school I can tell you, high windows, heavy iron desks, strict teachers always giving us the stick. I can remember one old teacher who used to take us for music. He used to walk up and down the aisles playing his violin, and if you were talking and not listening, he used to stop

104

and whack you across the head with his bow.

What a tartar he was! He'd bray you as soon as look at you. We used to be scared stiff of the teachers in those days; they used to be like gods to us. And we left school at fourteen, you know. We'd no choice, our parents couldn't afford to keep us at school. We'd to get out and get a job as quick as we could to help keep the family. It'd have made no difference if we'd passed the scholarship, our parents couldn't have afforded to send us. Not that it'd have made much difference to me. They had to blow the school up to get me out of standard three as it was.

WALLY Bet they have to blow this school up to get him off the stage.

Cut to a flashback:

The street

DANNY Weren't they terrible?

RONNIE They get worse.

DANNY If I was Manager of that lot the unemployment figures would be up by eleven on Monday.

RONNIE Twelve. Collins was no better when they brought him on in the second half.

DANNY Bastards! You'll be getting your bleeding heads kicked in.
We hear the Mayor's voice over

MAYOR Ay. Times were hard when I was a young man in the thirties. There was massive unemployment for a start . . . and even if you got a job you never knew how long it was going to last. They were hard times, but in some ways they were good times. People seemed to stick together more then, and we managed to have some good times in spite of all the difficulties.

The greenhouse

GEORGE Aye, we joined the Labour Party about the same time. But that's about the last thing we done together. I soon decided that that wasn't the way and I threw out. Joe went from strength to strength though. Became local secretary, got on the Council, and now look at him. But it finished him, Ronnie, he got respectable. He went soft. You should have seen the difference in the old days when we had any bother on with the management and we had to go and see them. In those days he was as hard as nails, principled in his arguments, he wouldn't budge an inch. But then he changed. You felt that he wanted to be at the other side of the table with them. And then he started to go off

105

for a drink with them afterwards. As though it was one big game, all pals together like. Well you can't do that Ronnie, it's war lad. And when I think of them lads in the moulding bay, at it from half past four in the morning, scuffling, non-stop with hardly time for their breakfasts sometimes. Callouses on their hands as big as eggs; burns on their arms from metal splashes. . . . It still makes my blood boil to think about it. Still there's one consolation. He can't do as much damage as if he were in the Union. Just think if they'd made him Sir Joe Brannigan. What a disaster that would have been for the lads.

The school hall

MAYOR You might not believe it to look at me now, but I was a real firebrand in those days. But as I got older I got more sense. And I came to realise that there were two sides to every question, and things are not always as simple as they might first appear. Nowadays with all the opportunities you've got almost anybody can get on provided he's prepared to work hard for it.

He smiles and sits down to applause.

Cut to a wide shot of group around Ronnie. He laughs. A master leans in, prods Ronnie, grabs his lapel, and sends him out of the hall.

We hear the audience rising, and the choir and audience singing "Jerusalem" over the following:

The school corridor

GEORGE Now then, what's up?

RONNIE I've been sent out.

GEORGE What for?

RONNIE Laughing.

GEORGE Now they wouldn't take kindly to that now, would they?

RONNIE It was Wally's fault. I couldn't help it.

GEORGE Well there's not much point in standing there is there? Mr Howard'll not have time to deal with you today.

RONNIE Mr Douglas said I'd got to wait here.

GEORGE You might as well come and give me a hand for an hour. I'll see Mr Douglas.

RONNIE All right then. Might as well.

GEORGE Come on, Ron.

Cut to a wide shot of part of the audience singing, then to a line of boys, pausing on the empty place next to Robson.

The singing of "Jerusalem" continues in the background as we cut to a long shot of Ronnie and George crossing the playground and passing the Mayor's car.

From the school we go to the steel works. In medium shot we see a man shovelling by a furnace. As he comes forward into a medium shot, we see that it is Mr Warboys.

Cut to the clothing factory, and close-up on Mrs Warboys machining.

Cut to Danny's factory, and a close-up of him inserting a steel bar into a machine.

Superimpose over the machine, whilst "Jerusalem" is still being sung in the background, the final credits.

The Piano
BBC 1
Stanley Reynolds

North Country comedy always seems to work best when it is spinning around one very simple idea. This is true of, say *Nearest and Dearest*, Grandada's knockabout Donald McGill seaside postcard series, or more serious stabs at realistic comedy like Julia Jones's *The Piano* on play for today last night on B.B.C. 1.

Here the comic idea was that Auntie Ada, played by Hilda Barry, was holding up the whole of a town's urban redevelopment by refusing to move out of her old house because the piano will not fit into the new council house. The joke was that the town's redevelopment was being done by her nephew Willie (Glyn Owen) who she had raised as her own son.

This is not perhaps the newest of dramatic ideas but it is enough to carry the viewer along and Miss Jones worked out a rather classical mathematical formula in which each character's attempt to solve the piano problem would be cancelled out by another character's objection.

Thus, when Willie wanted to put the piano in his own home Mabel, his bride of six months (Janet Munro), objected because it did not fit in with her modern decors and when Mabel suggested that they sell the piano to an antique dealer Willie objects because the dealer was his wife's old boy friend.

But more than the plot was Miss Jones's handling of the North Country characters: the hard headed old Auntie, the blustering Willie who stops wheedling and dealing long enough each week to play in the town's brass band. Miss Jones knows the North well and has a fine way with its talk.

There was one particularly good scene when Uncle Edgar (Leo Franklyn) is musing about the garden he will have in his new bungalow.

"Aye", says Auntie Ada, "everything comes to him who waits." "But it were a long time coming, Ada", he says. "Forty years", she says. "isn't long."

The North Country dialogue, however, has built-in dangers. One always seemed to get characters repeating themselves so that in the end one is in no doubt whatsoever about what a shining new town Willie wants to make out of the old slum streets or just how much Auntie Ada's old dad loved that piano. This unfortunately gave the play a comic aspect that the author did not intend.

But this was a moving and very well observed comedy with some excellent performances, particularly from Janet Munro and Hilda Barry as the opposing generations of northern women.

Hilda Barry

The Piano
Julia Jones

The Cast

Willie Duckworth
Mabel, *his wife*
Ada Ackroyd, *his aunt*
Edgar, *her husband*
Jeremy Plunkett
Ted
Enoch
Claud

The Piano

An aerial view of a new housing scheme. New houses rising beside the old ones being pulled down. The old streets are typical of a northern industrial town, narrow with little houses with front doors straight onto the street and a maximum of four rooms. In the distance new flats soar up into the sky and patches of green break the monotony.

The camera closes in on one of the old streets. We see a close-up of its name :

"Myrtle Street."

The camera moves down the street to the front of number ten. It has the usual gleaming white door step and bright brass knocker. The windows are half covered with the traditional lace curtains.

The curtain of the downstairs front window moves and a face peeps out. Close up of the face. It is that of a woman in her late sixties. She is small with white hair and bright sharp eyes.

Ada's front room

The camera goes into the room onto her as she stands looking out. She is dressed in her best cardigan and skirt and wears a pinny over it. The room is tiny with the front door opening straight into it from the street.

It is quite filled with an enormous grand piano and its stool. It is a monstrous thing from the middle of the last century but beautifully cared for and highly polished. Crushed into the only possible corner is a small music cabinet containing sheet music. Any movement in the room is difficult as there is only a narrow way between the piano and the walls. By very careful negotiation a person can move from the front door to the other door in the room, which leads through to the kitchen at the back. There is an old-fashioned cloth over the piano top and on it stands a photograph, an old faded one of a man standing to attention to have his photograph taken. The woman turns from the window and edges round the piano to pass through to the kitchen.

The kitchen

Cut to the woman as she walks through the kitchen to the scullery. The kitchen is cosy and old-fashioned. There is still a kitchen range, black-leaded and shining, with a brass fender highly polished. A couple of old

*armchairs stand on either side of the fireplace. There is a table in the
centre of the room with a day cloth over it. The dining chairs are tall
and old.*

*There is a big chest of drawers on the wall opposite the fireplace. A
grandfather clock ticks in the corner. The lino is highly polished and a
modern bright rug lies in front of the fender. There are cupboards built
in on either side of the range.*

The scullery

*Cut to the woman entering the little scullery. It contains a modern gas
stove and an old slop stone sink with only a cold water tap. She fills
a kettle and puts it on the stove.*

*The scullery stands at a right angle to the kitchen and the two windows
look out onto a backyard with a brick wall separating it from next door.*

The backyard

*The woman moves into the yard through the scullery door. Shot down the
yard. It is quite small opening into an "L" shape at the bottom. There
at the bottom is a man of about seventy. He is pottering among a lot of
plants and flowers in tubs. He is watering them, etc. He is in shirt sleeves
and no tie. His trousers are quite obviously his best and are held up with a
wide leather belt and an equally wide pair of braces. His boots are
brightly polished.*

ADA *(calling)* Edgar! *(He looks up at her.)* What are you up to?
The woman and the man speak in clear old Lancashire dialect.

EDGAR *(sighing)* Seeing to the plants.

ADA Eh?

EDGAR *(irritated and shouting)* Seeing to the plants!
*His movements are slow and careful, not just because of his age but
because he is a man like that.*

ADA Well, leave them alone!

EDGAR I've near finished now, Ada.

ADA You'll get that shirt dirty—

EDGAR I'll not.

ADA —and you know full well our Willie's due any time.
She bustles back into the scullery and through to the kitchen.

The kitchen

*Ada starts to get cups and saucers out from the cupboard and lay them on
the table.*

The scullery

Cut to Edgar entering the scullery.
He washes his hands at the sink.

The kitchen

Edgar moves through to the kitchen window drying his hands. He stands there looking down the yard.

EDGAR Times I've stood at this window—(*Ada stops what she is doing and looks at him. It is quiet in the room except for the clock ticking.*) Times I've stood here and looked down that yard—(*Ada joins Edgar at the window.*) Looked down and seen a garden.

ADA A garden? (*She looks at him as if he were mad.*)

EDGAR In the mind's eye Ada—in the mind's eye I've seen a garden—

ADA Oh.

EDGAR Spreading lawns and banks of flowers.

Pause while Ada looks down the yard too, trying to see with the mind's eye what Edgar sees.

ADA We've plenty of flowers Edgar.

EDGAR Aye—in pots.

ADA You've done wonders out there—(*Edgar sighs.*) Oh, but you have Edgar—best backyard in the town it is. And only a few more days and you'll have a real garden. (*Pause.*) From what our Willie says there's a lovely little garden to the new bungalow. (*Pause.*) Everything comes to those that wait.

Edgar turns round at this. Ada smiles up at him and he tries to smile back.

EDGAR It were a long wait.

ADA Only forty years.

Edgar moves to put the towel back in the scullery.

EDGAR Forty years married, eh?

ADA Gone in a flash.

EDGAR (*twinkling at her from door*) Seemed a bit long sometimes. Shall you miss it do you think?

ADA What?

EDGAR The old kitchen?

ADA No. (*After a slight pause.*) No Edgar, I won't. Clinging to the past—that's no way to live . . . and it's not been the same since Willie got married.

EDGAR It's not and that's a fact.

ADA And talking of Willie, we shall have him on us in no time at all.

EDGAR Plenty of time.

ADA We don't want to keep him waiting.

112

EDGAR We'll not do that.

Ada bustles into the scullery and puts the kettle on. She returns to put on a hat in front of a mirror over chest of drawers.

Edgar starts to put on a tie which he takes from one of the drawers.

ADA He's a busy man now.

EDGAR He always were a busy man.

ADA Since he got on the council he's had his hands full—

EDGAR He likes it that way.

ADA —and then there's all this building he does—

EDGAR Aye.

ADA —these lovely houses and bungalows he's putting up—

EDGAR Aye.

ADA —and his trumpet practice—

EDGAR Aye.

ADA —so there's no time to waste. (*Pause.*) Shame he couldn't stay over for his dinner.

EDGAR No time to waste.

ADA Don't be nasty, Edgar.

EDGAR Not nasty—he's a busy man.

He twinkles at her.

ADA I like to have him here for his dinner.

EDGAR He's got a wife now.

ADA That's what I mean.

EDGAR What?

ADA They don't take time to cook properly.

EDGAR Who?

ADA These bits of girls.

EDGAR Mabel's not so young.

ADA Young enough and flighty with it.

EDGAR Now, Ada—

ADA Willie wasn't the first—

EDGAR Did he have to be?

ADA And she's very funny wi' me.

EDGAR She doesn't say yes to you all the time, if that's what you mean.

ADA You know what I mean.

EDGAR I know you like your own way.

Ada looks at him and then moves huffily into the scullery, to warm the tea pot. She comes back holding it against herself.

ADA (*dreamily*) He were a lovely baby.

EDGAR A man now.

ADA A fine man too.

EDGAR Of course.

ADA Doing a lot for this town. Something to be proud of—our Willie.
She is staring out of the window, clutching the tea pot still. The camera comes out of the window, over the housing estates, and into the town proper. We see the crowded streets and smoking chimneys, then a block in the centre. Along the top of the building are huge letters saying: "William Duckworth Ltd."

William's office

We cut into the window at the top. A new modern window, long, to give a good view over the town. We move to the face of a man sitting behind a desk in a spacious office. There are a number of maps and plans of the town on the walls. He has a big folio of plans in front of him and is studying them carefully. He has an intelligent face with very shrewd eyes. He is quite a heavily-built man but not tall, typical of the stocky businessmen of the North.
There is a knock and the glazed door into the office opens and a young woman comes through, plain, but attractive and bright-looking, and with a good figure.

MABEL Willie.

WILLIE *(without looking up)* Aye?

MABEL Nearly time you were off.
He looks up at her and smiles, then leans back in his chair.

WILLIE Come here, Mabel.
Mabel smiles back and comes to the desk holding a note-book ready for notes. Willie indicates the plans lying on his desk. Mabel obediently looks at them. She looks a little puzzled as she takes them in and looks up at Willie, who beams back at her. He gets up and moves across to the window.

MABEL *(uncertainly)* Not the Myrtle Street development, is it?

WILLIE It's not at that. *(Willie's smile grows broader.)*

MABEL What then?

WILLIE What follows after.

MABEL After?

WILLIE After Myrtle Street.

MABLE Myrtle Street's not started yet.

WILLIE We shall be at the knocking down in a week or so.

MABEL Moving fast, Willie Duckworth.

WILLIE Past time someone moved in this town.

MABEL You'll frighten folks.

WILLIE Never.

MABLE They like to take their time.

WILLIE *(He looks out of the window obviously pleased with himself.)*

114

No way to get things done.

MABEL (*looking at the plans*) They seem very far-reaching.

WILLIE (*He turns back into the room.*) Eh?

MABEL These plans.

WILLIE They are far-reaching.

MABEL Cover a third of the town so far as I can see.

WILLIE No use in piece-mealing.

MABEL I don't follow

WILLIE Planning a bit here—a bit there—the whole place must be re-thought. (*He stands looking like the monarch of all he surveys. Mabel looks at him.*)

MABEL Willie—you're so wonderful.

WILLIE Oh—I don't know. (*She suddenly laughs at him.*) Mabel . . . come here. (*She crosses to him. He looks out of the window and draws her to him.*) Look at that.
The camera shows a shot of the vista of the town through the window.

MABEL Yes?

WILLIE I shall clear all that.

MABEL All what?

WILLIE I shall clear it all—little streets—pigsty houses—

MABEL (*shocked*) Willie!

WILLIE What?

MABEL Folks in this town are very clean!

WILLIE Speaking figuratively, I was.

MABEL You must watch what you say.

WILLIE Must I?

MABEL Don't want to offend, do you?

WILLIE Whether I offend or not I shall clear it—build a new town centre—shopping precincts—flats—and roads—big new roads circling the town to take the heavy traffic—cutting across the centre at chosen places—(*He is staring out of the window like a visionary. He looks back at Mabel.*) You can see the start of the roads on those plans.

MABEL Yes?
Willie walks back to the plans and looks over them and then stares at the window again.

WILLIE Best town in Lancashire I shall build—open space for folks to walk and breathe in—children to play—*Willie returns to the window and Mabel. They look out together for a moment.*

MABEL Pity—

WILLIE Mmmm?

MABEL I like the little streets and houses.

WILLIE You don't live in them.

MABEL I did once over.

WILLIE Not now. (*He looks at her approvingly for a second and then puts his arm round her.*) Not now, Mrs William Duckworth. (*He kisses her cheek with a smacking kiss.*)

MABEL Watch out!

WILLIE What for?

MABEL Breaking our rules!

WILLIE Oh, aye.

MABEL Made on our wedding day.

WILLIE No shenanigans in office hours.

MABEL So back to work—for two more minutes. (*They check their watches.*)

WILLIE (*going back to desk*) First-rate secretary, I've got.

MABEL First-rate wife?

WILLIE (*smiling at her and winking enthusiastically*) Right then—check programme for rest of day.
He takes out a notebook from his pocket and Mabel consults hers.

MABEL (*reading off*) First to your Auntie Ada's—

WILLIE Aye—

MABEL To collect her and Uncle Edgar and take them to see their new bungalow—(*She stops and looks up at Willie.*)—and I hope she likes it.

WILLIE Sure to.

MABEL She's a bit of a funny one.

WILLIE Not Auntie Ada.

MABEL (*thoughtfully*) Doesn't care for me.

WILLIE But I do—(*He looks at his watch.*)—and the two minutes is up, Mrs Duckworth—
Willie puts his arms round Mabel and kisses her.

MABEL (*emerging*) You daft lump, Willie—anyone could walk in.

WILLIE Not wi'out knocking—check rest of programme—
He opens his book again round Mabel's back and she looks at hers over his shoulder and starts to read again.

MABEL Take them home and then to the site to check wi' foreman—
Fade out on them as she reads.

Ada's kitchen

Cut to Ada's face. She is sitting in one of the straight dining chairs, her hat on and her handbag by her.
There is a knock on the front door. Ada jumps up and goes to the window looking down the yard.

The yard

We see a shot down the yard. There is Edgar in a mac and flat cap looking at his plants. Ada knocks on the window to him. He looks up and she beckons him to come in. He nods.

The front room

Ada moves to the front room and squeezes past the piano to the front door. There is another bang on the door.

ADA   Alright, alright!

Willie's voice calls through the letter box:

WILLIE   Look lively, Auntie.

ADA   I'll give you lively!

She opens the door to Willie standing on the step. He laughs down at her.

WILLIE   You took your time.

ADA   Came as quick as I could.

She opens the door to let Willie through and disappears behind it as she does so, re-appearing again as she closes it.

WILLIE   How are you, eh? (*He picks her up as if she were a child and kisses her on each cheek. Ada enjoys it, but speaks to him sharply.*)

ADA   Give over you great softy.

WILLIE   (*imitating her voice*) I'll give you "softy".

He sits her on top of the piano.

ADA   Willie!

Edgar half appears in the door from the kitchen.

EDGAR   Well, then, Willie.

He puts his hand to Willie and sees Ada, his jaw drops.

WILLIE   A nice day, Uncle.

EDGAR   What on Earth?

ADA'S VOICE   Willie—get me down from here.

WILLIE   Don't you like it up there?

ADA   Cheeky boy!

WILLIE   Come on then. (*He lifts her gently down.*)

ADA   What would your grandfather say?

WILLIE   Laugh. I don't doubt.

ADA   On his piano of all places.

She straightens the cloth of the piano and then her pinny.
Edgar and Willie move into the kitchen.

The kitchen

ADA   Mabel didn't come then?

WILLIE   A lot of work to get through.

ADA   She didn't mind you coming?

WILLIE Why should she?

ADA (*looking innocent*) I'll just pour the tea.

WILLIE Tea?

ADA Put us on till dinner time.

WILLIE I don't want tea—I'm a busy man—

ADA I know but—

WILLIE Why waste time on tea?

EDGAR Nervous—

WILLIE Never.

ADA Now, Edgar.

EDGAR Hardly slept a wink last night.

ADA Well—after all.

WILLIE What, Auntie?

ADA I mean—I've lived here since I were a baby—

WILLIE Time for a change then.

ADA And your grandfather before that.

WILLIE You've said yourself he were all for progress.

ADA Oh he was—he was—and I'm not holding back—I've always wanted a new house—

EDGAR Wi' no stairs—

ADA And a bathroom—

EDGAR Wi' hot and cold water—

ADA In the kitchen too.

EDGAR And a French window onto the garden!

ADA (*clapping her hands like a child*) You're a good boy, Willie—

WILLIE I do my best.

ADA Your grandfather'd be proud of you.

WILLIE Aye well, I've made a start.

EDGAR A first rate one at that.

ADA Since you got on that council, Willie, things have moved.

WILLIE A bit of vision's all that's needed.

EDGAR There's not many have it.

ADA His grandfather did! (*Edgar and Willie exchange looks again.*) Look to the future he'd say—look to the future—*Willie gets Ada's coat. With a decisive movement she goes to the door into the parlour.*

The front room

ADA I can remember—

WILLIE (*Willie is behind her with the coat.*) Auntie—

ADA I can remember when me and Jinnie were little girls.

WILLIE Your coat, Auntie—(*He starts to help her into it as she speaks, her eyes bright with memories.*)

118

ADA   He'd stand. . . . He'd stand at that front door looking out and he'd say—Ada—Jinny? All of you—the day will come when all these little streets'll be gone—all gone—and there'll be fine clean buildings wi' big windows to see out. A new town for folks like us—a new town wi' no smoke and pianos for all as wants 'em. (*Willie has managed to ease her into the parlour as she speaks and she finishes up by the piano. She looks down at it lovingly, and then freezes.*) Willie!

WILLIE   Eh?

ADA   The new bungalow.

WILLIE   Well?

ADA   How many rooms?

WILLIE   You know very well how many rooms there are—(*Willie's eyes light on the piano and a horrible thought begins to take shape. Showing in the expression on his face.*)
Bathroom—kitchen—bedroom—living room—

ADA   Is it a big living room?

WILLIE   A bit bigger than this.

ADA   The kitchen?

WILLIE   Very small—(*then hopefully*) with hot water and cold water.

EDGAR   (*very quietly*) Dear Lord—Dear Lord and Harry. (*He walks heavily through to the kitchen and leans on the mantelshelf.*)

ADA   You'll need to give us a bigger place Will.

WILLIE   I can't do that.

ADA   You can do anything you've a mind to.

WILLIE   Not that—the bigger places go to the marrieds.

ADA   We're married!

WILLIE   The young marrieds—they need them.

ADA   I need one, Willie.

WILLIE   They need them for families—

ADA   And I need one for . . .

WILLIE   Grandfather's piano—but it doesn't count as a child.

ADA   One more room'll do.

WILLIE   (*suddenly shouting*) I haven't got such a thing.
There is a pause.

ADA   I'll not move without it.

WILLIE   You're being childish, Auntie.

ADA   (*looks at him*) Our dad loved his piano.

WILLIE   I know—

ADA   We all learnt on it—save you—and I gave my word to see to it when he'd gone.

WILLIE   He wouldn't want you to miss a lovely new bungalow for it.

119

ADA I gave my word—

WILLIE A long time ago.

ADA No use to it—like I said—

WILLIE Just come and take a look.

ADA No use at all.

WILLIE You'll change your mind when you see it.

She looks at him proudly. Edgar appears in the door behind her.

EDGAR Come on lass.

ADA (*after a pause*) I suppose we might put it in the bedroom. *They both stare at her.*

EDGAR And sleep on it?

ADA Don't be daft! (*She glares at him very close to tears.*)

WILLIE Auntie—just come and take a look at the new bungalow and we'll think of the piano after, eh? (*She looks at him.*) I can't wait much longer—

EDGAR Indeed he can't we've held him up no end as it is.

WILLIE I've a lot to get through today and I'd like to be home for me tea.

ADA Well—

EDGAR Let's get cracking, Willie.

ADA I'll come—

WILLIE Away we go—

ADA But Willie—(*Willie stops dead by the front door, a look of apprehension on his face.*) Understand this—if there's no place in the new bungalow for your grandfather's piano there's no place for me! *She passes through the front door in front of Willie like a tiny battleship. Edgar follows looking miserable, and Willie gives the piano a dirty look as he closes the front door.*

The shot faces out on the piano, majestic in the little room.

A street in the town

Mabel is walking along one of the lesser streets in the town. She has her shopping basket on wheels and is humming brightly as she walks briskly along. She looks bright and happy and very efficient. She hesitates by a shop window and makes as if to go on and then finally gives way and looks in the window.

Shot of the name over the top: "Jeremy Plunkett"

Shot of the contents of the window. It is a music shop. The window is full of guitars and piano accordions, new and gleaming. Here and there is the odd wind instrument and at the sides, one or two second-hand instruments. There is a display of sheet music too. The window is well laid out with a certain feeling for the artistic. Shot of Mabel's face as she looks in. She is smiling to herself. Mabel is about to move off, when she is startled by a man's voice.

JEREMY Mabel Heatherington!

Mabel turns sharply and sees a man standing in the shop doorway. He is perhaps a little shorter than Willie and a tiny bit plump.

MABEL No.

JEREMY Eh?

MABEL You made a mistake, Jeremy Plunkett.

JEREMY What d'you mean?

MABEL Mabel Duckworth now.

JEREMY Oh aye.

MABEL And I have been for the past six months.

JEREMY (*There is a slight posh note to his Lancashire accent and there is an artistic note about his dress, though still retaining its northern quality.*) Six months too long.

MABEL Well, then?

JEREMY Sorry.

MABEL (*smiling*) How are you? (*Jeremy shrugs.*) You're putting on weight.

JEREMY Who cares?

MABEL It's not good to get fat. (*Jeremy shrugs again.*) You're not to let yourself go, Jeremy.

JEREMY Are you worried?

MABEL I'm fond of you.

JEREMY So you married Willie Duckworth.

MABEL Very fond—

JEREMY But fonder of Willie.

MABEL . . . and I don't want to see you go to pieces just because I left you.

JEREMY You're very sure of yourself, Mabel—

MABEL You need to be sure in this world and a man who can't get by without a woman is a poor sort of thing.

JEREMY You hard piece!

MABEL No.

JEREMY Make yourself indispensable and then come and talk like that!

MABEL Just being sensible.

JEREMY Cold and calculating!

MABEL I know what I'm after.

JEREMY The successful town planner and future mayor, eh?

MABEL If you like.

JEREMY And you got him!

MABEL Willie's a good man—

JEREMY Ambitious.

MABEL —doing a lot for this town.

JEREMY And himself at the same time.

MABEL (*after a pause*) You're jealous.

JEREMY Not of his success.

MABEL Then you're a fool.

JEREMY And he's a thief—stealing my girl.

MABEL I love Willie—

JEREMY Let's hope it stays that way.

MABEL —and I don't love you.

JEREMY Not what you said once over.

MABEL I—were very young then.

JEREMY Two years younger than you are now.

There is a pause. Mabel looks in the shop window and Jeremy watches her. She makes as if she will move off, but catches Jeremy's eye and so they stand, both caught up in a nostalgic moment.

JEREMY (*wistfully*) Long time since you were here.

MABEL Eight months—exactly.

JEREMY Yes. (*Pause.*) Care to look around? (*He indicates the shop with a movement of his head.*)

MABEL Anything interesting?

JEREMY An old bassoon.

MABEL I . . . (*Mabel looks away undecided. Making up her mind:*) I'd like to see it. (*She smiles at Jeremy.*)

JEREMY (*suddenly smiling back*) Come on, then. (*Jeremy's face lights up as he moves to his shop door and he looks very attractive. He opens it with his keys.*) Just going for a bit of lunch.

MABEL Won't hurt you to miss it.

She looks meaningfully at his figure. He smiles and she walks past him into the shop.

Inside the music shop

It is small and crowded with the usual accoutrements of a music shop. Mabel passes straight through like one who knows her way very well, into the back room of the shop. It is very different from the front parts of the shop. It is half display and half workshop and one corner has a tiny antique dining table and a couple of chairs. Mabel hesitates by the table for a moment and then moves past it. The instruments here are all odd. A spinet, beautifully cared for stands by the wall; a photo of Mabel stands on it. There is a lute and other old things and on a little work bench lies a bassoon. Jeremy watches Mabel as she walks round the room with a loving air. She stops by the spinet and raises its lid and tries a note.

JEREMY First time you come here—

MABEL You played it. (*Mabel looks at him, then looks away.*) Peaceful here.

JEREMY Can't think why you left.

MABEL Things to do in the world.

Jeremy looks at her puzzled and Mabel looks quickly away and sees the bassoon. She moves to it and picks it up.

JEREMY (*going quickly to it*) Careful.

He takes it handling it gently.

MABEL Old John Thistlewaite's?

JEREMY (*surprised*) The same!

MABEL Played it all over Lancashire. And his father before him.

JEREMY How did you know?

MABEL Willie used to blow on it.

JEREMY Willie?

MABEL After old John's wind was gone—Willie used to blow it for him— liked to hear its voice John said.

JEREMY I didn't know Willie played a bassoon.

MABEL You know very well he's first rate on the trumpet.

JEREMY A trumpet's not a bassoon.

MABEL It's all blowing, isn't it?

JEREMY (*Jeremy looks at her. He lays the bassoon down.*) Blasted Willie!

MABEL Why?

JEREMY (*shrugs*) Always does the right thing.

MABEL He knows what he's up to. Will you sell it?

JEREMY I hope not.

MABEL D'you ever sell anything? (*She smiles a little mischievously.*)

JEREMY (*He smiles back at her.*) Not if I can help it.

MABEL You don't change.

JEREMY I—don't care for change.

MABEL (*She sits on a piano stool and looks around.*) No.

JEREMY You look tired.

MABEL Oh?

JEREMY (*exploding*) Damn big bull!

MABEL Who?

JEREMY Willie.

MABEL What about him?

JEREMY Wearing you out!

MABEL We suit each other.

JEREMY I suited you once over.

MABEL As a friend.

JEREMY (*he looks at her, shocked*) More than a friend.

MABEL (*looking away*) Depends—how you look at it.

JEREMY Everyone said you'd marry me!

MABEL (*shocked*) Then they'd no right to—

JEREMY They'd every right!

MABEL (*getting up*)—for I make me own mind up about things! (*Jeremy turns away.*) Time I—were off. (*Jeremy does not move.*) Jeremy—

JEREMY Well?

MABEL I never made any promises. (*Pause.*) I never once *promised* you anything. (*She moves across to the door. Then turns back to look at Jeremy with a certain wistfulness. He has not moved.*) Now—mind you watch your weight—(*Jeremy turns on her.*)—Girls don't go for fat men.

JEREMY There's only one girl for me.

MABEL There's plenty more fish in the sea.

JEREMY Only one like you.

MABEL I should hope so! But there's plenty near enough you could marry.

She goes through the door and the shop door bangs, but Jeremy does not move. He crosses to the bassoon and looks at it and then turns from it in disgust. Fade out on his morose face.

Willie's living room

Fade in on Willie's face. It is also morose. The camera pulls back to bring in the room. It is a typical room in a small modern house. L-shaped with a dining alcove leading into a well-equipped kitchen with a serving hatch. All is new and modern in contrast to Jeremy's room. It is very tastefully furnished with the latest in modern furniture.

Willie is seated on a couch with his trumpet. He blows a few solitary mournful notes. Then he puts it down and wipes his lips and looks at his watch. He swears gently under his breath and goes into the kitchen and puts the kettle on. He moves back into the living room with a lost air. Then he hears the sound of a key in the front door. It opens and bangs to and the sound of steps are heard in the hall.

WILLIE Mabel?

Who else? (*She comes into the room with her basket.*)

WILLIE You're late.

MABEL Shopping—and you're early.

WILLIE Band practice tonight—I've put the kettle on.

MABEL (*Mabel crosses the room to him and drops a kiss on his face.*) Good.

WILLIE I'd like me tea.

She looks at him a little surprised at his lack of response. She then takes

124

off her coat and goes through to the kitchen with basket. Willie picks up his trumpet and shakes the spit out of it and tries another note. Mabel comes from the kitchen carrying cups. She looks at him.

MABEL You look tired.

WILLIE I am tired!

MABEL (*Mabel looks at him and then turns back to kitchen. She stops by a mirror on the wall.*) Do I look tired? (*Looks round at him.*) Do I look tired, Willie?

WILLIE Haven't noticed it.

MABEL (*He makes as if to blow his trumpet, but Mabel speaks looking back into the mirror.*) Jeremy said I looked tired.

WILLIE (*Willie stares at her.*) Eh?

MABEL Jeremy Plunkett said I looked tired.
She goes into the kitchen. Willie gets up slowly and goes to the kitchen. He stands in the doorway looking at her.

Their kitchen

WILLIE When did you see Jeremy Plunkett?

MABEL (*starting to cut bread and butter*) Doing my shopping.

WILLIE That why you were late?

MABEL Oh, no.

WILLIE Where did you see him?

MABEL At his shop.

WILLIE What—were you doing at his shop.

MABEL Walking past. (*Pause.*) Does she like it?

WILLIE Eh?

MABEL Auntie Ada—does she like the bungalow?

WILLIE Of course.

MABEL Thank heaven for that.

WILLIE How did you come to be talking to Jeremy Plunkett?

MABEL He spoke to me. (*Pause.*) When does she move?

WILLIE Who?

MABEL Auntie Ada.

WILLIE She doesn't—what did he say?

MABEL Jeremy?

WILLIE Who else?

MABEL He's got John Thistlethwaite's bassoon.

WILLIE He showed it to you?

MABEL Yes.

WILLIE In his shop.

MABEL Yes.

WILLIE (*into kitchen*) Now listen to me, Mabel—

MABEL Well—?

The living room

She goes through to the living room with bread and butter and puts it on a little table. Willie follows her.

WILLIE You're to stay out of that shop.

MABEL I like that shop.

WILLIE I'll not have you in that shop.

MABEL But—

WILLIE No buts.

Mabel smiles at him and returns to the kitchen. She gets out the jam and takes it to the living room.

MABEL What d'you mean she's not moving?

WILLIE Auntie Ada.

MABEL Of course. (*She goes into the kitchen and warms the teapot.*) Well? (*She stands in the door looking at Willie.*)

WILLIE Grandfather's piano . . . (*Mabel stares. She goes back and fills the teapot, then comes back into the room.*) Won't fit into the bungalow.

MABEL Oh my lord. (*She puts teapot down, pours two cups and hands one to Willie.*) She'll have to move . . . won't she?

WILLIE She'll not move without the piano.

MABEL Then she'll *have* to fit it in somewhere.

WILLIA Can't be done.

MABEL It'll have to be done.

WILLIE (*Willie looks at her.*) Can't be unless they eat their dinners off it. (*He spreads jam on bread.*)

MABEL Well . . . if she won't move she must just stay where she is.

WILLIE Bang smack in the middle of a great new housing scheme?

MABEL It looks like it.

WILLIE Are you my secretary?

MABEL Yes.

WILLIE Then talk sense.

He eats his bread and jam. Mabel sips her tea looking squashed for the first time.

WILLIE Right spanner in the works.

MABEL The piano?

WILLIE Right blasted spanner in the works.

MABEL Perhaps—

WILLIE What?

MABEL You'll be able to get Auntie Ada to—see sense.

WILLIE She's stubborn.

MABEL Still you—

126

WILLIE Very stubborn—you know she is—

MABEL Yes I do.

WILLIE Very stubborn.

Fade out on his face eating bread and jam. Miserable.

Ada's scullery

Fade in on Ada's face. She is washing dishes at the slop stone sink. In the scullery Edgar is drying. They wash and wipe in silence. At last Edgar speaks.

EDGAR Ada—(*Pause.*) Ada—you've not said a word since Willie left us.

ADA Nowt to say.

EDGAR All afternoon you've not said a word. It's a lovely little place, Ada.

ADA Oh?

EDGAR A fine little bungalow—all Willie said about it—airy—light—and a first-rate garden.

ADA That's all you care about.

EDGAR Nay.

ADA All you care about—your garden.

EDGAR Nay Ada—that's not fair.

ADA I've yet to see what else you care about.

EDGAR Ada!

ADA You're very selfish, Edgar Ackroyd.

EDGAR I never thought to hear you say that to me. (*Pause.*) Any road—

ADA What?

EDGAR It's no use.

ADA (*challengingly*) What's no use?

EDGAR That danged piano.

ADA That's a very nasty thing to say.

EDGAR You know it's no use, Ada—

ADA I do not!

EDGAR You were at banging on it at Christmas and there's hardly note'll play properly

ADA Nowt to do wi' the piano.

EDGAR What then?

ADA Just my fingers—grown stiff.

EDGAR (*sighing*) I'd be glad to be shot of the thing.

Ada looks at him. She has finished the dishes and now dries her hands and leaves the scullery. She moves into the kitchen and sits down. Edgar finishes the last dish and looks at Ada sitting in the kitchen like the goddess of grief. He throws down the tea towel.

Ada's kitchen

EDGAR   Well hell and tommy, Ada—forty years married and first chance I've had of a garden.

She doesn't move. Edgar picks up the tea towel and hangs it up. His old hands are trembling.

ADA   Our Dad loved that piano.

EDGAR   He's had his day—and so's the piano.

ADA   Bought it out of his own sweat he did—brought it home the day he were wed—took the window out to get it in. Our mother told me.

EDGAR   Poor woman.

ADA   Taught himself to play—and all us children too. He'd lovely fine hands from the weaving and they'd fly over the keys. "Our Chopin" Mother called him. There was none of us could ever play like him. (*Pause.*) I thought Willie might once over—but he'd no heart for it. It were a great grief when he took up wi the trumpet.

EDGAR   Ada—the piano were finished when it came time for Willie to learn.

ADA   Never.

EDGAR   Drove him mad—all out of tune.

ADA   He'd no patience.

Edgar walks to the window and then back across the room.

EDGAR   Great monster.

ADA   Willie?

EDGAR   That danged piano! Sitting there—doing nowt.

ADA   It'd hurt our Dad to hear you talk like that.

EDGAR   He's dead—and has been for the past thirty years—

ADA   Makes no odds!

EDGAR   —and I wish he'd taken his piano with him.

ADA   Edgar!

EDGAR   Coming between us and a lovely new home.

ADA   No home at all—

EDGAR   A first-rate garden.

ADA   No sort of place if there's no room for a piano!

EDGAR   If it's a piano you want why don't we get a little new one?

ADA   There's only one piano I want—

EDGAR   We've enough in the bank.

ADA   —and I'll not move without it!

Their front room

Edgar moves into the front room. He stares at the piano.

128

EDGAR For two pins I'd—
        He half lifts the piano stool.

The kitchen

Cut back to Ada. She is crying quietly. Edgar comes back and sees her. He sits in a chair at the far end of the room and watches her, helpless in front of her tears, fade out on Ada's face.

A band rehearsal-room

Cut to a goup of men's faces all laughing. There are three of them. A tall thin man in his forties. A wheezing thick set man and a small neatly made man—both the latter in their fifties. The camera pulls back to bring in the whole room. Seats and music stands are arranged for a band to play, with a dais for the conductor. A number of men are standing about or sitting in their places chatting. One or two enthusiasts try the odd notes. Cut back to the group. Jeremy is just joining.

TED Jeremy—
JEREMY Ted—(*He nods at the other two men speaking their names.*) Enoch—
        Claud.
CLAUD (*wheezing heavily*) No, wind tonight Jeremy.
JEREMY Just have to be content wi' listening, Claud.
CLAUD Aye.
JEREMY (*There is a certain authority about him not usually evident.*) Are we
        ready?
ENOCH Waiting on Willie.
TED Not usual for him to be late.
CLAUD No—
        *The door swings open and in comes Willie. He removes his coat at the
        door and exchanges greetings with the men as he walks across to the group.*
ENOCH Mabel keep you?
WILLIE (*looking at Enoch*) I'm ready when you are.
TED You look a bit off.
WILLIE Oh?
TED Very off.
JEREMY Don't blow if you're not up to it.
WILLIE (*looking at him*) I'm up to it.
TED Mabel been giving you the once over?
        They are all moving slowly towards their places.
ENOCH Want watching these young wives.
CLAUD Start as you mean to go on, Willie.
WILLIE Mabel's alright. (*Willie and Jeremy catch each other's eyes and
        immediately look away.*) Going well with Myrtle Street, Ted?

129

TED   Our side of it, Willie.

WILLIE   Good.

TED   Folks are shifting out nicely—top end's clear.

WILLIE   I saw it were today.

TED   You'll be at the knocking down in a week or two.

WILLIE   Soon as we get the all clear.

JEREMY   Poor old Myrtle Street.

WILLIE   It's had its day.

TED   Condemned these past five years, Jeremy, and nothing done till Willie got things moving.

JEREMY   Moves too fast for some. (*Willie looks at him to see what exactly he means but his face is a blank.*) Folks had their homes there.

WILLIE   Poor sort of homes.

JEREMY   A sad thing to be uprooted.

WILLIE   We can't all live in the past.

JEREMY   There's some just like to take their time.

WILLIE   If you had your way we'd still be living in caves.

      There is an undercurrent to their words and Ted steps in to break it.

TED   They're ready to go, Jeremy.

JEREMY   Think so?

TED   I know so.

ENOCH   He ought to—been on the housing since he were a lad.

CLAUD   And Willie builds grand homes.

WILLIE   I do my best.

JEREMY   Aye—you're moving up.

WILLIE   Better than moving down.

JEREMY   Always were a pusher—

TED   Jeremy—

JEREMY   Right through school you were a pusher—

WILLIE   I get things done.

JEREMY   At what cost?

WILLIE   Someone must look to the future.

JEREMY   And to hell with the present?

WILLIE   You're a bigger fool than I thought you to be.

JEREMY   I love this town.

WILLIE   Sentimental tripe!

JEREMY   And the people in it.

WILLIE   The people in this town—the young people—are getting out as fast as they can—looking for go-ahead places—for decent homes—for well-run factories—I'm building a place they'll want to stay in—I'm building—

JEREMY   You see nowt but bricks and mortar!

WILLIE   I see a new town wi' sunshine and green places—wi'—

JEREMY   And yourself on top?

WILLIE   (*dangerously quiet*) It's not an easy job—and it can be unpleasant
—if there's anyone fancies it and can do it better than me they're
welcome.

JEREMY   Chance is a fine thing.

WILLIE   It were a fair vote put me in—try your hand at the next election.
There is a pause. The two men eye each other.

ENOCH   Past time we were at our blowing lads.
*The tension continues. Jeremy is the first to waver. His eyes drop and he
gets out his baton from his pocket. He takes his place on the conductor's
dais and taps at his stand. The men take their places, Willie with the
rest. Jeremy raps again and raises his arms. The music starts. Willie
blows a blast on his trumpet. Jeremy takes no notice and raises his arms
and the music starts.*

Willie's house

*Cut to Mabel, reclining on the couch watching television. The lighting
is dimmed and all looks modern and very up-to-date. Mabel looks well
content. The front door bangs and Mabel sits up. She shakes her hair
and smooths her dress and Willie enters the room. She waits for him to
come and kiss her but he hardly notices her, just looks round the room and
then switches off the tele and puts on the main light. He is preoccupied.
Mabel shrugs and goes into the kitchen.*

MABEL   (*calling*) Coffee?

WILLIE   Mabel—

MABEL   Yes?

WILLIE   Come here. (*She returns.*) I reckon we can manage it.

MABEL   Manage what?

WILLIE   The piano.

MABEL   What d'you mean?

WILLIE   Get it in here of course.

MABEL   In here?

WILLIE   Aye.

MABEL   I knew you'd think of that.

WILLIE   (*pleased*) Well then.

MABEL   I felt in my bones you'd think of that.

WILLIE   Just about get it in nicely. (*He doesn't look at her but walks about
the room weighing up positions for the piano.*)

MABEL   I won't have it.

WILLIE   (*Willie stops now and looks at her.*) Grandfather's piano?

MABEL   I won't have it in my home.

WILLIE Our home.

MABEL Our home then—

WILLIE It's a lovely piano.

MABEL Auntie Ada may think so.

WILLIE Antique.

MABEL I don't care for antiques.

WILLIE You lived wi' 'em long enough—

MABEL I hate antiques.

WILLIE Wi' that Plunkett chap.

MABEL —and I hate the piano.

WILLIE It'd hurt Grandfather to hear you say that.

MABEL You sound like Auntie Ada.

WILLIE We're very like.

MABEL And any road—you hate it too.

WILLIE I could try to like it.

MABEL I couldn't.

WILLIE Then you'll have to put up wi' it.

MABEL I won't.

WILLIE If you put up wi' all that junk of Jeremy Plunkett's to suit him you can put up wi' grandad's piano. To suit me!

MABEL What about my television.

WILLIE Move it.

MABEL There's nowhere else it'll go.

WILLIE Find a place.

MABEL No!

WILLIE You're very sharp, Mabel!

MABEL Willie—you like modern things?

WILLIE Of course.

MABEL Clean modern lines—

WILLIE Yes.

MABEL And so do I.

WILLIE Well?

MABEL We planned our home like that.

WILLIE We did.

MABEL I love our home.

WILLIE So do I.

MABEL And I won't have it cluttered wi' antique pianos that gather dust!

Their kitchen

She sweeps into the kitchen and bangs about with a coffee pot and coffee.

WILLIE Nowt else to do Mabel.

MABEL Auntie Ada must look to her own piano.

132

WILLIE Auntie Ada is sitting in the middle of my housing scheme.

MABEL So?

WILLIE Any hitches and it'll hold up all my plans.

MABEL Don't you care about anything else?

WILLIE What else?

MABEL I—I—I—

WILLIE We start clearing Myrtle Street in a week or so—folks must all be out by then.

MABEL Then you must give her a bigger house.

WILLIE Can't be done.

MABEL Why not?

WILLIE They're not for old folks as well you know.

MABEL You could give Auntie Ada one.

WILLIE I'd have the whole town on me back wanting to pick and choose. Besides she's my Auntie.

MABEL What difference does that make?

WILLIE Looks like favouritism.

MABEL You're making a mountain out of a mole-hill.

WILLIE Auntie Ada's no mole.

MABEL I wish she were.

WILLIE Now then.

MABEL I knew she'd give trouble.

WILLIE She's a right to want Grandfather's piano.

MABEL But no right to thrust it on to us!

WILLIE Don't be so childish, Mabel.

MABEL Childish?

WILLIE Childish and petty.

MABEL I'm sticking up for myself.

WILLIE I cannot waste time on trifles like this!

MABEL I've a right to a nice home.

WILLIE And I've a right to some co-operation!

Mabel pours water on their coffee. Then she stops.

The living room

Willie goes back into the living-room. Mabel appears in the kitchen door.

MABEL Jeremy Plunkett!

WILLIE (*jumping up*) Dear Lord and Harry!

MABEL But Jeremy—

WILLIE Mabel—I've a terrible temper—

MABEL But—

WILLIE I've a terrible temper when I'm roused and if I hear that name once more—

MABEL But he might help.

WILLIE Help?

MABEL He could buy the piano!

WILLIE No!

MABEL If you asked him.

WILLIE Ask Jeremy Plunkett?

MABEL Yes.

WILLIE Me—ask Jeremy Plunkett?

MABEL Why not? He goes for that kind of thing.

WILLIE I'll go for you if you mention his name again.

MABEL But, Willie—it solves everything!

WILLIE I'd not ask owt of that Plunkett blighter if he were the last man on earth!

MABEL I'll ask him then.

WILLIE (*nearly exploding*) I've warned you Mabel—

MABEL You're being childish—

WILLIE *I'm* being childish?

MABEL For a forward-looking man you're very primitive.

WILLIE Mabel—if you go near that man it'll be the end of our marriage.

MABEL You do care about our marriage then?

WILLIE Say no more!

MABEL Because Willie Duckworth if I have to come down each morning into this room and face that piano, there'll be no marriage!

WILLIE I thought you liked music.

MABEL *Some* music.

WILLIE You like my trumpet.

MABEL Willie—if that piano comes in—I go out.

We fade out on her determined face.

Myrtle Street

The knocking down has started. We cut to the wall of a half-demolished house. There is a shout and the wall crashes down. A cloud of dust rises.

Ada's back yard

Cut to Edgar in his back yard with his plants. He is wearing an old fire-watching helmet. Dust and bits fall on him. He curses quietly. A couple of umbrellas have been placed so that they cover some of the plants. He lays down his watering can and fixes an umbrella so that it protects a plant better. Ada appears at the top of the yard, and sweeps up the bits there.

ADA (*calling*) How far have they got?

Edgar steps up on an orange box placed for that purpose against the wall,

134

holding his helmet to give him maximum protection as he does so. He looks over the wall.

EDGAR Number fourteen's outside wall.

ADA Getter nearer. (*There is the light of battle in her eyes.*)

EDGAR Too danged near.

There is another rumble and Edgar crouches to escape the bits.

The kitchen

Cut to Ada going into the kitchen. There is the patter of plaster falling from the front room.

Ada's front room

Ada looks in. The piano is covered with bits. She sweeps them off and returns to the kitchen. She rummages in a drawer and brings out a white sheet. She covers the piano with it. There is a knock at the door and Ada squeezes round the piano. She peeps out of the window. Shot of Ted standing on the step. He sees Ada at the window and touches his hat to her. She opens the door and peeps round the door at him.

ADA Well, Ted Houghton?

TED Still here then?

ADA What else?

TED Top of the street's all down.

ADA Oh?

TED You know it is.

ADA Why tell me then?

TED They'll be at this one tomorrow.

ADA They'll not knock this house down.

TED It's scheduled.

ADA We're not moving.

TED You're booked to move, Mrs Ackroyd.

ADA I'll move when you give me a bigger house, Ted Houghton.

TED Not up to me, Mrs Ackroyd—and you can't stay wi' everything coming down round you.

ADA I can't see why not.

TED It'd be dangerous.

ADA Dangerous?

TED Things falling.

ADA I'll take my chance.

TED Just trying to put you in the picture.

ADA Well just mind your own business and leave me to mine.
(*She slams the door.*)

TED (*through the letter-box*) We can put you out you know. We've a right to put you out.

Cut to Ada on other side of the door.

ADA *(shouting back)* There's no one'll put me out and you can tell the council and our Willie that I said so!

Cut to Ted. He shrugs and moves off. Cut back to Ada as she places the piano stool in front of the door. She looks at it and then goes to the kitchen.

Ada's kitchen

Edgar is just entering from the scullery. Ada takes a chair and struggles through to the front door with it.

Their front room

Edgar watches, following her through. She rests it against the front door.

EDGAR Who was it came?

ADA Ted Houghton.

EDGAR From the housing?

ADA That's right. *(She looks triumphantly at the chair and the stool.)* There's no one'll put me out.

Edgar stares at her and goes through to the kitchen.

Their kitchen

Ada follows.

EDGAR Daftest thing I've ever known. *(Ada takes no notice. Edgar brushes bits off himself, and takes off his helmet.)* Worse than the blitz. *(Ada starts to clear up bits of plaster that have fallen in the kitchen.)* Damn piano gets more consideration than your own husband.

ADA You can look after yourself.

EDGAR And will do too!

He moves into the scullery and washes his hands.

The scullery

ADA *(following him)* What d'you mean by that?

EDGAR I mean that if you won't shift I will.

ADA *(after a pause)* On your own?

EDGAR On me own.

ADA Leave me you mean?

EDGAR I do.

ADA Where would you be without me?

EDGAR In a fine new bungalow—*(There is another rumble.)*—and no rumbles.

ADA Edgar—

EDGAR *(drying his hands furiously)* What?

ADA Edgar—I—(*Then briskly.*) I'll make a cup of tea.

EDGAR And keep the plaster out of it if you can.

Ada fills the kettle and Edgar moves into the kitchen and sits in his arm-chair at first brushing off a bit of plaster. Ada comes and stands looking at him. Then she moves and picks up the bit of plaster he brushes onto the floor. Edgar opens a newspaper.

ADA I—(*Edgar doesn't move*). I never thought you'd desert me.

EDGAR You never know your luck.

ADA All these years together and now you talking to me like this. (*Edgar throws down his paper.*)

EDGAR Damn and set fire to it, Ada I like a bit of comfort and any road—

ADA What?

EDGAR They can make us go, if they've a mind—

ADA (*fiercely*) There's no one'll make me do owt I don't want to!

EDGAR Don't talk so daft, woman!

ADA And I tell you, Edgar Ackroyd, that if they do I'll not forgive you and I'll put the piano in the new living room.

EDGAR It'd not go through the door.

ADA I'll break the door down.

EDGAR And be in court for spoiling council property.

ADA You're on their side, Edgar—after all these years, you're on their side.

EDGAR I'm on me own side and trying to get us out of here wi' some dignity and no piano.

ADA I shall never leave our Dad's piano.

EDGAR Kettle's boiling.

ADA So you can just make up your mind to it and when Willie comes on Sunday for his dinner I shall tell him once and for all that it's a bigger house or we stay put!

She sweeps into the scullery. Fade out on her determined face as she warms the tea pot in the scullery.

Willie's house

Fade in on Mabel's determined face. She is putting on a Sunday hat in front of the wallmirror in her living room. There is the faint sound of church bells from outside. Willie is sitting on the couch in his coat, staring at his trumpet. There is a certain stiffness between them. Willie sighs.

WILLIE Well then—

MABEL What?

WILLIE Only one thing for it—

MABEL Oh?

WILLIE Means we shall have to cut down a bit—

MABEL What does?

WILLIE I shall have to buy them a house.

MABEL Buy them a house?

WILLIE Big enough to take that blasted piano.

MABEL *You'll* buy them a house?

WILLIE Nowt else for it.

MABEL Very philanthropic.

WILLIE No need to be funny. (*Pause.*) If I don't shift 'em soon I shall be a laughing stock.

MABEL No!

WILLIE All my big plans for this town and I can't manage me own Auntie.

MABEL She takes some managing.

WILIEL (*getting up*) Don't start, Mabel.

MABEL I—

WILLIE I've had more than enough this past week and I'd like a bit of peace on me one day off.

MABEL They're very proud.

WILLIE They'll have to swallow it this once.

MABEL And stubborn.

WILLIE So are you for that matter.

MABEL I don't see why I should spoil my home for the sake of a broken-down old piano.

WILLIE No.

MABEL After all it's not as though Auntie Ada's ever been nice to me.

WILLIE She's an old lady.

MABEL And over-fond of you.

WILLIE She's been good to me—and look sharp now or we shall be late and you know she hates to keep the dinner waiting.

Mabel is about to speak but Willie's expression stops her. Fade out on her face.

The scullery

Fade in on Ada's face. She is standing over her stove making gravy in the meat tin. Edgar is standing near to her sharpening a carving knife on a steel. Edgar starts to cut at a joint of beef. A piece of plaster floats gently down into the gravy. Ada tut tuts as she fishes it out. Edgar sighs.

ADA Oh stop your wittering, Edgar!

EDGAR Well what a place to ask folks to.

The kitchen

Willie and Mabel are sitting at the table which is laid for Sunday dinner. Mabel is staring straight in front of her and Willie is fiddling with a fork. There is a self-conscious silence. A piece of plaster floats down and Willie and Mabel watch it without moving or changing their expression. It lands on the table and Willie flicks it away. He glances at Mabel, but she is staring through the window.

ADA *(calling)* Ready now.
She comes through with vegetable dishes. Edgar follows carrying the meat. He lays it on the table to finish the carving.

MABEL *(very politely)* Can I help?

ADA *(equally politely)* Nowt to do now.
She returns to the scullery and they sit in silence while Edgar goes on carving. He looks thoroughly miserable. Ada returns carrying the gravy boat and a dish of yorkshire pudding. She waves the pudding under Willie's nose who smiles obediently. She sit sdown. Edgar hands her a plate with meat and Ada piles vegetables onto it.

MABEL Is—that mine?

ADA Yes.

MABEL That's plenty then. *(Ada cuts into the yorkshire pudding.)* Not for me, thank you. *(Mabel smiles sweetly as Ada hands her the plate.)*

ADA *(cuttingly)* Beef without Yorkshire's nowt.

MABEL I like it that way.
Ada takes another plate and piles stuff onto it. She puts a huge slice of Yorkshire onto it. She passes the plate to Willie who receives it without visible emotion. Ada watches him anxiously.

ADA Don't wait. *(Willie looks at the plate and smiles weakly at Ada. Mabel and Willie start to eat but Willie toys with his dinner.)* Eat up, Willie.

MABEL *(coldly)* He's not a child.

ADA Eh?

MABEL I said—he's not a child.

ADA I don't recall I said he was.

MABEL He doesn't need to be told to eat up.
Ada puts vegetables onto the next plate with a certain viciousness.

EDGAR Watch out *(Ada looks at him.)* You know I can't abide carrots.
Ada scrapes the carrots off the plate. Then hands it to Edgar. She takes the last plate and lays it down in front of her and sits there. They try to ignore her for a moment but at last Edgar has to speak.

EDGAR Are you not hungry?

ADA Not now.
He tries to eat again. Willie tries to. Edgar lays down his knife and fork

at last and looks at Ada.

EDGAR Ada—

ADA Well?

EDGAR How can I sit here eating and you like that?

ADA Like what?

EDGAR All uppety and touching nowt.

ADA It's coming to something when I can't speak to a lad I brought up like me own. (*Willie sighs and lays down his knife and fork giving Mabel a dirty look.*) When I can't open me mouth in me own house.

MABEL (*calmly*) It's not your house.

ADA I'd like to know whose it is then?

MABEL You should have been out days ago.

WILLIE (*pushing his plate from him*) Mabel!

ADA You've put Willie off his dinner now.

MABEL He was off it before I spoke and it'll do him no harm.

ADA He needs his food!

MABEL In moderation.

ADA I—

WILLIE Give over.

ADA Willie, I'll not have—

WILLIE (*getting up from the table*) I'm like a shuttlecock between the pair of you.

ADA That's not my fault.

EDGAR Cannot we just eat our dinners in peace?
Willie comes back to the table.

MABEL Why don't you tell her Willie?

WILLIE In my own time Mabel.

ADA Tell me what?

WILLIE Eat your dinner, Auntie.

ADA Tell me what, Willie?

EDGAR Oh tell her, Willie lad, for we shall have no peace until you do.

WILLIE Just something I've decided.

ADA About the house?

WILLIE Yes.

ADA You've got a bigger one for us?

WILLIE Not yet.

ADA (*triumphant*) There I knew you could do anything you wanted to! (*She beams all round.*) When do we move?

WILLIE Just as soon as I can put the money down.

EDGAR Money?

WILLIE A deposit.

140

ADA Buying a house?

WILLIE That's the idea.

MABEL Big enough to take that.

She indicates the front room with a nod of her head. There is a pause. Edgar lays down his knife and fork very carefully and wipes his mouth on his napkin.

EDGAR We've no money for a house, my lad.

WILLIE (*smiling brightly*) But I have.

MABEL Easy for Willie to raise capital.

ADA I'm sure it's very kind of you—but—

WILLIE No buts, Auntie—

ADA I'm sure I don't know—

EDGAR I do.

Edgar gets up and moves to the window and looks out.

WILLIE What, Uncle Edgar?

EDGAR You'll buy us no house.

WILLIE It'll have a garden.

EDGAR If it has a dozen gardens you'll still not buy it.

Mabel quietly lays down her knife and fork and looks at Willie. She is a little fearful.

WILLIE The sensible thing to do, Uncle.

EDGAR Not for me.

ADA Edgar—if Willie—

EDGAR I'll have no charity.

WILLIE (*Willie moves to Edgar and stands behind him.*) Not charity, Uncle.

ADA He's our own kin.

EDGAR Makes no odds.

WILLIE You can pay me back.

EDGAR (*looking at him with scorn*) Tha knows we'll pay nowt o' it back at our age. (*He turns back to the window.*) All my life I've paid my way—

WILLIE I know, Uncle—

EDGAR Worked hard and paid my way and I'll not have it different now.

ADA Edgar—

EDGAR And nor will you, Ada—or if you do you'll have wi'out me.

WILLIE This is silly, Uncle—

EDGAR Don't rile me, Willie.

WILLIE It's a reasonable suggestion—

EDGAR I'm a mild man and I'll put up wi' a lot—but I'll not take charity.

WILLIE Can you tell me what else there is to do?

141

EDGAR Move into the bungalow—

  ADA No!

EDGAR (*looking at her*)—which is ours be rights.

MABEL Of course.

EDGAR And put the piano where it belongs—

  ADA Now then.

EDGAR —in the knackers yard!

  ADA That's a terrible thing to say.

EDGAR It's a terrible thing—

  ADA Eh?

EDGAR —that piano—a terrible thing—ruled our lives since the day we wed.

  ADA You've never spoke like this before.

EDGAR Then it's past time I did.

  ADA (*looking round lost*) Willie—what am I to do?

WILLIE (*despairingly*) I've told you both what to do.

MABEL Why not put it in store?

  ADA What?

MABEL The piano—why not put it in store?

  ADA Our dad's piano in store?

MABEL Just until you sort out at the new place.

  ADA I'll not put it in store!

WILLIE Why not?

  ADA It'd be the death of it!

EDGAR It'll be the death of us before we're finished.

  ADA Don't talk daft.

EDGAR It will—if you don't buck up your ideas and come to your senses.

  ADA (*desperately*) I see no reason why Willie shouldn't buy us a house if he wants to.

EDGAR Have you no pride, woman? Or has that damned thing driven you quite out of your mind?

WILLIE Now don't quarrel—

  ADA He's getting old, Willie—

EDGAR (*stricken*) Ada!

MABEL (*She goes to him and touches his arm. She turns to Ada.*) You're very selfish, Auntie Ada.

  ADA Eh?

MABEL I said you're selfish.

    Edgar moves proudly from Mabel back to the window. She watches him with great sympathy.

  ADA Who are you to call me selfish?

142

MABEL   Aren't you?

ADA   A chit of a flighty girl like you—

WILLIE   Now mind what you say—

ADA   I know what I'm saying and any road I don't see her helping out at all—

MABEL   If you think I'm having that hulking monster in my house—

ADA   I wouldn't dream of letting you have it—

MABEL   That's what you want I know—

WILLIE   Mabel—you've said enough.

MABEL   I've not started yet—

WILLIE   Then stop before you start.

MABEL   I've a right to my say.

WILLIE   Not now.

MABEL   *She* can say what she likes of course—you don't care about me—

WILLIE   Mabel—grow up—

MABEL   (*looking at Ada*) It's not me wants to grow up!

ADA   I'm more than twice your age young woman!

MABEL   You don't act like it!

WILLIE   Mabel—I don't care to hear you talk like that.

MABEL   (*ignoring him*) You're making Willie a laughing stock!

ADA   Me.

MABEL   Yes.

ADA   I never am!

MABEL   He said so!

ADA   After all I've done for him! (*She stares at Willie.*)

MABEL   Bosses him—bossed him all his life—

WILLIE   Mabel—

ADA   Now see what sort of a wife you've got.

MABEL   —and Uncle Edgar and anyone else as'd let you!

WILLIE   Shut up, Mabel!

MABEL   Somebody ought to tell her!

ADA   I don't wish to have anything to do wi' you.

MABEL   You don't show it!

ADA   You lured Willie into marriage.

MABEL   What!!

ADA   And I've put wi' you just so far as I am able—

EDGAR   Ada—will you watch your tongue!

MABEL   Willie—will you say something.

WILLIE   I want nowt to do wi' it—as far as I know we're discussing grandfather's piano—

MABEL   You're going to let her get away with what she's said about me—

WILLIE   Give over, will you!

143

ADA   I said that girl'd give trouble—I said it, Willie—I said—

WILLIE   Both of you give over! Nattering away!

ADA   Willie—

WILLIE   I thought you were all for progress—

ADA   I am!

WILLIE   You can't see further than your own four walls!

ADA   Your grandfather—

WILLIE   Build new homes they all say—build new homes—but let's keep the old 'cos we don't like change!

ADA   That's not fair—

WILLIE   Well I tell you, Auntie, if you're not out of this house be the end of the week I'll serve a sheriff's warrant on you and have you moved by force!

ADA   You're own Auntie!

EDGAR   Now then, lad—

WILLIE   And you're as bad as her—

EDGAR   I—

WILLIE   You and your daft pride—

MABEL   Pot calling the kettle.

WILLIE   Eh?

MABEL   On about pride.

WILLIE   Well?

MABEL   Couldn't ask Jeremy Plunkett—

Willie stands quite still for a moment staring at Mabel. Then he gets his coat. When it is on he looks round them all.

WILLIE   I've said my say—you know what to expect—the council have their rights too—and so do the folks who *want* decent homes. (*No one moves. Willie opens the parlour door.*)

Just think things over, and when you've all come to your senses you can let me know.

He goes. The front door bangs. Still no one moves. Edgar slowly reaches for his cap by the mantelpiece and puts it on and then winds a scarf round his neck. He goes out into the yard. Shot of him walking down it to his plants. Shot of Ada's face tired and hurt. Shot of Mabel's face, uncertain and very young suddenly. She makes a move to clear the table. She picks up a plate.

ADA   (*very straight and proud*) Put it down! (*Mabel puts it down.*) When I need your help I'll ask for it.

Mabel looks as if she might speak but is quelled by Ada's look. She stands not knowing what to do or say and finally gets her coat and hat. She looks at Ada whose face doesn't relent one bit and then finally she goes very quietly. The front door slams. Ada is very still. She looks at the table.

ADA A lovely dinner—gone to waste.

Edgar enters from the back yard. He doesn't look at Ada. He goes to the old dresser and opens the top drawer. He takes out some ties and socks and lays them on top. Ada watches him.

ADA Edgar—what are you up to?

EDGAR Packing.

ADA Packing?

EDGAR Packing my bag, Ada.

ADA No.

EDGAR I shall move out tomorrow with or without you.

ADA But—

EDGAR To the new bungalow. (*He goes to the stairs which lead up from behind a wooden door in the corner. He opens the door.*)

ADA Edgar—you've no bed.

EDGAR I shall sleep on the floor.

ADA And catch your death?

EDGAR I'd rather catch it that way than choke on Willie's charity.

He moves up the stairs and the sound of his heavy steps and the creak of the stairs echo through the kitchen. Ada stays still and then moves into the parlour.

Their front room

Ada looks at the piano and then picks up the photo.

ADA Such a peaceable man—such a very peaceable man.

Fade out on her face for the first time, looking very old.

Willie's office

Fade in on Willie's face. Camera back. He is standing by the big window of his office looking out. It is dark and neon lights flash across his face. He is tired and drawn-looking. The office has the neat empty weekend look. No lights are on save for a tiny desk light. He is quite still and still in his coat. He sighs and moves across to the wall maps of his plans. He switches on a wall-light and looks at them. Then suddenly making up his mind he switches off the light and moves quickly to the door. He hesitates there and then goes off quickly.

The music shop backroom

Cut to Jeremy Plunkett working in his back room. He is wearing a flowery short dressing gown and velvet trousers and is working on the bassoon. The little table is laid with the remains of a meal and an antique coffee pot stands there. He is drinking coffee from a beautiful china cup.

There is a ring at his shop door bell. He looks up puzzled and then there is another ring and he moves through to the door.

The music shop front part

Jeremy opens the shop door and there is Willie. They stare at each other.

WILLIE Aye—it's me.

JEREMY What in merry hell?

WILLIE Can you spare a minute?

JEREMY Can I . . . what for?

WILLIE A—short talk.

JEREMY *(after staring at him)* Come in.

WILLIE Aye—

Jeremy stands aside and Willie goes through and waits in the shop for him. Jeremy locks the door and then they again stand and stare at each other.

JEREMY *(at last)* Go through.

WILLIE Thanks.

He moves into the back room and Jeremy after him.

The back room

Willie stands in the middle of the room looking big and clumsy. Jeremy moves to a photo of Mabel on the spinet and turns it face down. Willie has seen it.

WILLIE Too late. *(Jeremy shrugs. Willie looks round the room.)* Bit of a back water.

JEREMY I like the back waters.

Willie looks round with a certain interest. Then looks puzzled.

WILLIE How she . . .

JEREMY *(after a pause)* What?

WILLIE Nowt. *(He looks at Jeremy with a mildly puzzled air then he sees the bassoon. He goes to it and picks it up.)* Old John's?

JEREMY She told you?

WILLIE Oh yes. *(They look at each other and Jeremy looks away.)* You've done a good job. *(He examines the bassoon.)*

JEREMY I generally do—with those sort of things.

WILLIE *(trying a note)* A fine note.

JEREMY One of the best.

WILLIE *(laying it down)* Poor old John.

JEREMY Is that what you came for—the bassoon?

WILLIE No. *(He looks around the room again.)*

JEREMY Coffee?

146

WILLIE Aye. (*Jeremy pours some.*) Didn't realise it were such a back water.

JEREMY I didn't ask you to come.

WILLIE No—sorry. (*He takes the cup and wanders away from Jeremy's eyes again. He stops by the lute and tries a note.*) Might learn one of these one day. (*Jeremy waits. Then he goes to the bassoon and starts to work again. He is very carefully and lovingly cleaning it. Willie watches him.*)

JEREMY Well?

WILLIE (*by the lute again*) D'you reckon—

JEREMY Reckon what?

WILLIE (*Willie plucks a string. Then he straightens up and looks directly at Jeremy.*) D'you reckon you might buy a piano?

JEREMY A piano?

WILLIE A grand piano—antique.

JEREMY How antique?

WILLIE Seventy or eighty years.

JEREMY No good.

WILLIE Fine condition.

JEREMY The notes?

WILLIE I—no—not the notes.

JEREMY I thought not.

WILLIE Well?

JEREMY Not worth the space they take up. I wouldn't waste time or money on one.

WILLIE I'll put up the cash.

JEREMY Some shady deal?

WILLIE Nowt shady about my deals.

JEREMY Shady enough when you took Mabel.

WILLIE All fair and square, Plunkett.

JEREMY Not to my way of thinking.

WILLIE If you can't keep your women—

JEREMY Crude bastard!

WILLIE I—didn't come to row wi' you.

Willie moves round to the spinet. He is about to lift the lid.

JEREMY Not that!

Willie looks at him. He closes the lid and shrugs. Jeremy returns to cleaning the bassoon. At last he speaks, his curiosity getting the better of him.

JEREMY This piano—

WILLIE Yes?

JEREMY Is it famous at all?

WILLIE Infamous.

JEREMY I mean—anyone well-known play on it?

WILLIE Only Grandfather. (*He smiles a little. Jeremy looks up at him.*) Aye, you're right—it's Ada Ackroyd's. (*Jeremy watches him.*) Won't go into her new place.

JEREMY (*A smile begins to dawn on Jeremy's face. Willie moves away.*) So that's it.

WILLIE Is it?

JEREMY I heard there were some hold up at Myrtle Street. (*He starts to laugh. Willie shrugs.*) So she won't shift, eh? (*Willie moves away to the lute keeping himself calm with difficulty.*) Willie Duckworth the great builder—the great town planner—Willie Duckworth pushing to the top—can't shift his own Auntie—how are the mighty fallen. . . .

    Jeremy's laughter grows. Willie concentrates on the lute and gradually Jeremy's laughter stops and he wipes his eyes and blows his nose.

WILLIE (*looking at him*) Have you done?

JEREMY No wonder you look sick.

WILLIE I don't enjoy coming here.

JEREMY Lowering yourself eh?

WILLIE Not a very nice way to put it.

JEREMY Sacrifice even your pride to your ambition.

WILLIE Blast my pride!

JEREMY Oh?

WILLIE And it's not ambition—

JEREMY What then?

WILLIE I want to put this town on its feet—give it a future—

JEREMY Big words.

WILLIE And I want to hurt as few folks as possible in the process.

JEREMY Difficult.

WILLIE So it seems.

    Willie finally makes for the door.

JEREMY (Why pick on me) (*Willie stops with his hand on the door.*) Must be hundreds of ways you can shift someone.

WILLIE Piano means a great deal to her.

JEREMY So?

WILLIE She might let it come to you knowing you like such things.

JEREMY You're a clever man.

WILLIE Thanks.

JEREMY Always find the right thing to say.

WILLIE Not always.

JEREMY Where would I put the piano?

148

WILLIE Wouldn't be for long—she's getting on.

JEREMY Anything to get her moved eh?

WILLIE She'll have to go one way or t'other—I'd like her to go comfy.
Pause.

JEREMY A very clever man.

WILLIE (*suddenly bursting out*) Oh! Stop it, Plunkett, you've had your little triumph—now you can spread it all round—and—

JEREMY I'll look at the piano.

WILLIE (*staring at him*) Now?

JEREMY If you like—
Fade out on the two men looking at each other.

Myrtle Street

Edgar's anxious face. He is standing in the empty, demolished Myrtle Street staring down it and looking lost. A car's headlights pick him up. It stops by him and Willie pokes his head out. Jeremy is sitting by him.

WILLIE Uncle Edgar . . .

EDGAR Willie!

WILLIE What is it?
Willie gets out of the car.

EDGAR Ada . . .

WILLIE What about her?

EDGAR Went out over an hour ago and not come back.

WILLIE I'll take you home, Uncle. (*He pushes Edgar gently into the car.*)

EDGAR Ada. . . .

WILLIE I'll find Ada.
Willie gets in and they drive off. Fade out on Edgar's anxious face looking out.

Ada's front room

Fade in on Ada's face. She is in her coat and hat, standing looking down at the piano, her hand resting on it and her thoughts are miles away. The front door opens and Edgar squeezes in followed by Willie and Jeremy, hovering in the background.

ADA I were just thinking how our Dad'd sit here after he'd come from his work and make the notes sing. He'd fetch a new piece sometimes and be at practising it for hours until he got it right.

EDGAR Ada—you had me worried to death—

ADA (*sharply*) Have you been out wi' out a coat Edgar?

EDGAR Looking for you.

ADA I only just went for a walk.

EDGAR But gone so long.

ADA A lot to think about.

WILLIE Auntie—

ADA You here too?

WILLIE Aye.

ADA Come back then?

WILLIE Of course.

ADA And who is this with you?

WILLIE Jeremy Plunkett.

ADA Oh—I've heard of you. (*Jeremy smiles at her but Ada doesn't smile.*)

WILLIE He'd like to take a look at the piano.

JEREMY If I may, Mrs Ackroyd.

ADA Why must you look at my piano, young man?

WILLIE He—might find a place for it.

ADA What sort of a place?

JEREMY Well if it's worth anything

ADA Worth anything?

JEREMY I'm interested in antiques.

WILLIE Part of his business, Auntie.

ADA I see.

WILLIE So if he might just look it over—

JEREMY I shan't harm it.

ADA No.

WILLIE But . . .

ADA There's no money can buy this piano.

WILLIE Just let—

ADA (*with great dignity*) No Willie—it's not for sale to anybody even
if they thought it worth the buying . . . which it's not . . . ther's
nowt in the notes now.

JEREMY It's just possible, Mrs Ackroyd—

ADA Not now, Mr Plunkett.

EDGAR If this young man can help, Ada—

WILLIE It's worth a try—

ADA Don't look so worried, Willie.

WILLIE But—

ADA I'm beaten—

EDGAR No—Ada I—

ADA First time in my life I'm beaten, Will—

WILLIE Never.

ADA Not by you or by the council—but by Edgar—

WILLIE Edgar?

Edgar turns away.

ADA He's packing his bag.

EDGAR (*muttering*) Nowt else to do.

ADA I don't blame him.

EDGAR Ada—I'll not—

ADA A man needs his pride. (*Pause.*) But our dad were a proud man too, Mr Plunkett. He loved this piano . . . sweated for it—and there's no stranger'll look it over and take it out of pity.

JEREMY I—

ADA He'd have no charity either. So you can knock the house down Willie and the piano wi' it. I'd rather I knew its end than it mouldered away in some back yard to be broke up when I'm dead. (*There is a pause. No one moves.*) Well, then. (*She picks up the photo and puts it in her handbag.*) Well then—that's it—we move on tomorrow—and now I'll put the kettle on—you'll drink a cup of tea wi' us, Mr Plunkett? I reckon we could all do wi' one.
She moves to go to the kitchen. Fade out on her straight back.

Willie's house

Cut to Mabel's back. She is standing by the window of her living room looking out. The room is lit by a small light. She is waiting and watching through the window.

Willie's car

Cut to Willie and Jeremy in the car. It is just stopping outside Jeremy's shop. The men sit still for a moment and then Jeremy looks at Willie. Willie is dropping in his seat a little.

JEREMY Maybe you should try the backwaters for a while. (*Willie looks at him.*) Anyway—sorry.
Willie shrugs. Jeremy gets out and the door slams. The car drives off. Fade out on Jeremy's watching figure.

Willie's living room

Fade in on Mabel again. She hasn't moved. A car draws up outside, the headlights sweeping across the room. Mabel turns expectantly to the door and waits. The front door opens and closes. Then Willie enters. He takes off his coat without looking at Mabel. She waits. He sits on the couch staring in front of him. Then he gets up and gets a drink from a cupboard and pours a glass for himself. He raises the bottle in Mabel's direction without looking at her.

MABEL No. (*He sips his drink.*) Willie—(*Pause.*)—Willie—I've been thinking—(*Pause.*)—we could fit it in—Willie—for a while—(*Pause.*) Perhaps buy another house later on—(*Pause.*).

WILLIE (*he looks at her at last*) Too late. (*Pause.*) Blasted piano!

MABEL Eh

WILLIE Like a bomb—going off in our faces—

Cut to Mabel's face watching him not knowing what to say.
Cut back to Willie's face hurt and tired.

Myrtle Street

It is bright daylight. Myrtle Street is quite flat and from the remains of number ten a grab lifts the piano high in the air, a leg dangling and broken, and crashes it down onto a waiting lorry.

Ada and Edgar's new house

Mix from the piano, crashing onto the lorry, to a close-up of grandfather's picture. Ada is holding it and looking at it. The camera includes the living room of her new bungalow. She is standing in the centre of it looking at the picture. The old furniture from the kitchen is arranged incongruously in the room. Ada looks small and lost. She looks about her and then tries the photo on the window ledge and then somewhere else. It doesn't look right anywhere. She looks helplessly about her then and walks firmly to the old chest of drawers. She opens the top drawer, looks at the picture again and then puts it in the drawer and closes it with an air of finality.

The titles come up as she opens the french window and walks with a very straight back down the garden to Edgar who is busily replanting his pot plants. Fade out on them as they stand looking down at the plants.

The Camera Script

The authors wrote these plays with the television camera in mind, but the director still has the job of planning the exact camera positions, angles of shot, and sequence of cuts. Before rehearsals start, he therefore adds to the script fairly detailed camera and other technical instructions, as shown on the next two pages. This list explains some of the main camera and editing terms used:

ANGLE The direction and height from which the camera takes the scene.

CLOSE-UP A picture which shows a fairly small part of the scene, such as a character's face, in great detail so that it fills the screen.

CUT To change suddenly from one picture to another. This is done by switching from one camera to a second camera which is picking up a different scene or ANGLE of the same scene.

DISSOLVE To FADE one picture from the screen at the same time as a second picture is FADED IN. For a moment, then, the two pictures are MIXED on the screen.

FADE To increase the brightness of a picture so that the blank screen gradually fills with the picture (FADE IN). A scene can be ended by FADING OUT: the picture grows dimmer until it leaves the screen completely.

MIX As DISSOLVE.

PAN To swivel the camera whilst it remains in the same base position. It is therefore able to follow the movements of a person, or survey part of a room. (So called because the camera gives a "panoramic" view.)

SHOT The ANGLE or viewpoint given to the camera. A LONG SHOT, for instance, is taken with the camera a long way from the person or object being shown (or using a lens which gives this effect). This type of shot shows people as fairly small, but includes much of the background.

TRACK To move the camera forwards, backwards, or sideways.

ZOOM To focus quickly from a LONG SHOT to a CLOSE-UP whilst the picture is actually being shown. (This is done by using a zoom lens which can be re-focussed whilst in use.)

MONTAGE A series of fairly short, disconnected shots, run together so that they make a sequence, creating a general impression.

This page is divided into two halves

Vision ↓   *Sound* ↓   *Heard "over" the sounds of the room*

Medium shot

8. M.S. MRS WARBOYS   *Right*
    AT IRONING BOARD.
    TELEVISION PLAYING. "National Anthem".
    SHE PAUSES TO LOOK OFF (R) TO TV
    BRUSHES BLAZER PUTS IT ON A HANGER.
    CAM PANS HER L TO HAND IT BELOW
    SHIRT ON DOOR
                    Right
    CAM PANS HER (R.) TO SWITCH OFF
    TELEVISION SET. SHE PAUSES
    A MOMENT AT THE WINDOW:
    SHE TURNS AWAY.

                Very long shot
    CUT TO
9. V.L.S. HIGH ANGLE OVER EARLY
    MORNING TOWN:
    ZOOMING BACK THRO' WINDOW
    FRAME

10. L.S. MILK TROLLEY ON BALCONY
    MILKMAN DELIVERING MILK
            Wide shot
11. W.S. PARENTS BEDROOM.
    MR. WARBOYS REACHES OUT
    TO STOP ALARM:
    GETS OUT OF BED COMES TO
    CAM R. CALLING TO DANNY:

12. INT. BOYS BEDROOM
    2S
    DANNY GETS UP
    STARTS TAKING OFF PYJAMA

13. CLOSE GROUP SHOT MEN
    ARRIVING AT WORK:
    SEE MR. WARBOYS GO BY
    R TO L. IN CS

"Two shot" - we just see the two in the shot.

— 2 —

"NATIONAL ANTHEM"
over
INT. WARBOYS SITTING ROOM
NIGHT
            interior

"National Anthem"
Ends

The camera pans to hold her in the centre of the picture as she moves.

EXT EARLY MORNING
Exterior [all shots are labelled as "Interior" or "Exterior."]
Sounds of milk bottles

INT. WARBOYS BEDROOM

Alarm clock ringing

MR. WARBOYS: Come on Danny –
Let's be havin' yer...

Knocking on door.

Danny – come on Danny – lets
be 'aving yer.

EXT. FACTORY

The picture starts as a medium shot of the room, and then goes close so that Ronnie's sleeping face fills the screen.

Medium shot — 3 —

Inside the factory where Danny works

14. M.S. DANNY CLOCKING IN
PANNED R TO L.

INT. FACTORY/DANNY'S

15. M.S. RONNIE
ASLEEP.
ZOOMED IN TO C.S.

INT. BOYS BEDROOM

Noises over

We can still hear the noise of the factory as we see Ronnie in bed.

16. L.S. FLATS
PANNED R TO L.

PANNED DOWN PICKING UP
RONNIE IN W.S. COMING
TO CAM.

EXT FLATS

Ronnie is on his way to school and the detailed way of photographing him has been worked out: from a long way away the camera is to sweep across the flats from Right to Left. Then it focusses onto Ronnie who walks toward the camera.

17. MCS RONNIE GOING PAST
CAM R. TO L.

18. W.S. STEEL FURNACE
TRUCK COMING FROM FURNACE
PULLING OUT AND MOVING AWAY
INTO L.S.

INT. STEEL FACTORY

"close two-shot"

19. C2S MAN MR. WARBOYS DRINKING
TEA

20. C2S MEN L. FRAME

21. C2S MAN/WARBOYS with paper

MR. WARBOYS: What about this
two pound limit on rises then,
Joe?

22. CS MAN R

Each camera "shot" is numbered for reference in rehearsals.

— 3 —

Each page is numbered, top and bottom, so that everyone working in the studio can easily keep their place.

Thinking about Television Plays

Our television screens are filled with an average of 25 hours of drama every week. Audiences, particularly for some of the *series*, are as high as fourteen million. More people see the single performance of a separate play than saw *all* of Shakespeare's plays during his whole lifetime. Some of the characters from series and serials become, for good or for ill, household names.

Television drama, in fact, is huge in quantity. (Beside it the "live theatre" seems tiny—only about 2 per cent of the adult population, it is reckoned, visit the theatre.) But what does all this acting add up to? Does it mean anything to viewers, or is it just a way of pouring away time? Are these plays worth *thinking* about, or only gawping at? Anyway, what makes a "good" play? Is one person's opinion as fair as another's? Are phrases like "Great", "Crummy", "Boring", "All right" as accurate as it is worth getting in expressing opinions?

Enjoying and judging

As with most things worth enjoying so with plays: the more you think about your opinions the more enjoyment you can get. We all have opinions as we watch a play on television; we may stick to those opinions however many other people try to argue us out of them. But it is unlikely that we will keep them in exactly the same form. To exchange opinions requires us to have reasons for our ideas, and to be able to back up our opinions with these reasons. When we sort out our reactions in this way, ask ourselves *why* we feel this is a dull play or *why* we found that a moving ending, we sharpen our enjoyment. We may well find that this examination and the swapping of opinions leads us to alter slightly our first opinion.

Plays and Life

Drama is not life itself, although the style of television acting and play production often makes it seem almost as if it were. The camera work and set-building in, for example, the police station in *Reasonable Suspicion* would produce an effect on the screen that would be rather like a documentary programme on real police work. But drama is *about* life. We expect a good play to ring true, so that we feel: "Yes, people are like that!" or "Yes, they might well do that." Sometimes the writer will extend our understanding by showing people with characters that we could

156

not have imagined before. But we still have to be convinced by the play that people *could* be as they are shown to be by the author. If the author makes his characters too good to be true (too bad, too silly, or too weak, for that matter), we know that he has lost touch with life.

The characters we meet in plays need constantly to be compared in our minds with life as we know it. In this way we can judge:

Would Ada be as upset about the piano as she is in *The Piano* ?

Would the Headmaster in *Speech Day* really get 5GI to do so many chores?

Would the manager's wife make as much fuss of Paul as she does in *A Right Dream of Delight*?

We don't need any special knowledge or learning to answer these questions; we just need to compare what we see on the screen with what we've seen around us, and to wonder whether what we see of a character at the start of a play could lead to what we see by the end.

The writer's experience

A writer often builds his plays round snippets or whole sections of his own experience. Sometimes it may be no more than the setting or atmosphere which the writer uses as the backing to his story. Barry Hines taught for a while in a school. We do not know how much of the play, *Speech Day*, came from that, but he must have remembered a number of details. Similarly, Jeremy Seabrook trained and worked as a social worker before taking up writing. No doubt when he was doing that he heard of a number of cases of old people who did not want to be moved when large-scale redevelopment was going on. Possibly he even knew such a family at close hand, and he could even have been responsible for sorting out such a problem. Whether he actually met such a case or not, there is no doubt that he used some of his experience as a social worker to give him background knowledge, and possibly he even used a person he met or had heard of as the basis for Ada. No doubt ideas, characters, feelings, even snippets of dialogue in these and the other plays have all come from writer's observation, experience, or memory.

The writer's ideas

But the plays in this volume, and all the worthwhile plays on television, are more than just memories; the writer aims to do something more than just serve up experience and share it with the viewers. We could look into it this way: What makes the writer choose *this* story? What is it that interests him especially about *this* series of events? Often the answer is that the story seems to him to have some importance beyond the events that it shows, to have some wider "meaning".

Edgar's love of his plants in the yard of his small terrace house is an example of a detail that has a wider meaning. The author is, surely, suggesting that many people cherish something natural and beautiful, however cramped and limited their own living conditions. When Ada gives in, allowing Edgar to have a garden for flowers and giving up the piano with its memories, it is as if the author is asking us to consider whether creating beautiful, living things, isn't better than basing one's life on past memories. This "wider meaning" of the plays is part of what is meant by the phrase "true to life".

The author's attitude

We all have a sense of values which makes us feel that *this* is good and *that* is bad; we like certain people and not others; we admire and try to copy one way of behaviour and not another. An author shows *his* attitude by the way he writes about his ideas and characters. He invites us, so to speak, to sympathise with certain characters and to despise others:

Does Barry Hines expect us to like Ronnie Warboys?

Does Richard Harris expect us to admire either Pooley or Neil?

Does Julia Jones expect us to like Willie?

It may be difficult in some cases to give a clear-cut "yes" or "no". Willie, to take the last example, is shown as talkative, self-centred, and proud; but his author seems to have affection for him as well as some scorn.

We can then ask ourselves whether we share the author's attitude. If we can't share it and if we feel differently about the characters, we can try to see why. If there seem to be strong reasons for not sharing the author's attitude, then we obviously do not think he has written a good play. If, for instance, we think that Willie in *The Piano* is *just* an ambitious power-hungry and unfeeling man, we clearly don't share the writer's attitude, and he hasn't persuaded us to. We must, then, judge the play to be poor. Or if we find Doris in *A Right Dream of Delight* in all ways admirable, we clearly don't think much of the play as a whole.

Of course, an author may persuade us to *change* our attitudes. He may portray an apparently unlikeable character so that we can't help feeling some admiration or sympathy. In *Reasonable Suspicion*, for instance, we surely change our feelings towards Fred Pooley, Neil, and Ken Ridgeway more than once in the play. Both Neil and Fred Pooley are shown to have less admirable sides to their characters as the play goes on, and we probably feel that Ken is wiser and more sensible than either by the end. In *The Piano* we are shown two sides of each of the main characters, so that sometimes we sympathise with them, and at other times we see their weak points.

The way the characters speak

A play is a whole piece of writing, and it is dangerous to pick out aspects of it to think about separately. But when you are thinking about a play, it is sometimes helpful to do this all the same. The language that the writer puts into the characters' mouths is one of the most important ingredients of the play. A good playwright has a sharp ear for patterns of speech, and the different ways in which different people speak. In fact every speech should be "in character". Read over these two extracts from the plays:

"Oof, I damn near come a cropper on the ashphalt then. Biggest wonder out I never broke me ankle. Get mine, will you, Gerry at dinner-time, I might be a bit late."

"Bought it out of his own sweat, he did—brought it home the day he were wed—took the window out to get it in. Our mother told me. Taught himself to play—and all us children too. He's lovely fine hands from the weaving, and they'd fly over the keys. 'Our Chopin' Mother called him. There was none of us could play like him."

Even though television is so obviously a *visual* art, the dialogue in a play is possibly its most important single ingredient. Listen for dialogue that is effective, in character, and expressive. Both these speeches catch the speaker's character in the words used, the kinds of sentences, and the general style of the speech.

Written for television

There are many different ways of producing a play: the stage, the radio, film, television, even the puppet theatre. Each one ("medium" is the technical word used) has its own special difficulties and its own advantages. Producers are always experimenting, and it would be stupid to think that the details of how a television play is produced now are necessarily fixed for ever. Television is a fairly young medium, and is affected by a number of influences that are not really connected with the artistic use of the screen: the need for vast audiences, the necessity of keeping down costs, and so on. At the moment almost all television drama is "naturalistic"—that is, productions try to give the impression of being photographed actuality, as if they were documentary programmes.

When we have seen a television play we can consider whether it was well thought of in terms of television methods. There is no need to have a great deal of background technical knowledge to decide this. The important point is that the camera and the screen are more *selective* than the human eye. People see a wider span with their eyes than a camera can with its lens. At first this may seem a disadvantage for the camera—it cannot capture the impressiveness of a wide sweep of countryside, for instance. The camera concentrates attention on fairly small areas; so in thinking about the artistic use of television ask yourself whether this limitation is exploited as an advantage. Is the relatively narrow vision of the camera *used* or does it just seem a drawback?

The most obvious use is the close-up which can force our attention onto details at key moments, particularly of a character's facial expression. The author and director *choose* these moments. The viewer can ask, "Have they chosen them well?"

A human being combines the ability to pick up sights and sounds. The television machinery splits these two, using cameras for the first and microphones for the second. This splitting is obviously a complication, but, again, it can be *used* as an artistic device. For instance, the screen can show one person, whilst we are hearing the words of another person, *Speech Day* ends in this way. We *see* the members of the family at work, but we *hear* the school. This is an example of the author *using* television to help make a point in the story.

Some of the scenes in a television play are in fact filmed outside the studio at an earlier date than the performance. This is done because certain types of background, particularly outside scenes, cannot be well reproduced in a studio. But filming can be more than just a way of solving the difficulty of a cramped television studio. It also can be *used* for special effect. A series of separate filmed moments can be joined together to create a summary of an important part of the play. In *The Piano* the author needed to show the demolition of the street. This was done by a montage sequence in this way.

As a last example of the ways in which the technique of the television studio can be used to make the author's point, consider the way in which the ability to switch from one camera to another is used to take us suddenly from one incident to another. A scene can be broken off at the *dramatically* effective moment, without the necessity to round off a sequence. These cuts need not be just a mechanical way of getting a story along.

The plays to choose from

Television is called a "mass medium" because masses of people need to be interested in a programme if it is to be broadcast. Although a popular novel might sell many thousand copies, a book publisher would cover his costs if a novel sold as few as, say, three thousand copies. (Many more people might read the book in library copies of course.) But an audience of this size would be thought of as disgracefully small for television, mainly because of the immense cost of production (£6,000 an hour) and the few programme channels available. The BBC draws its income from licences which all set owners pay—and therefore it must appeal to a large audience. The ITV companies draw their income from paid advertisements, and the firms will only advertise if programmes are seen by large audiences.

The result is that television programmes have to be designed to attract large audiences. This means two things:

Audiences must not be frightened away by difficult, disturbing, or thought-provoking plays.

If possible the "habit of viewing" must be established.

Both these demands lead to formula writing, which we see particularly in series programmes. In these long-running huge-audience programmes a set pattern is established and viewers become accustomed to their favourite characters doing roughly similar things week after week. A few surprises are planted in each week's "play", but the author must be careful to keep up the cosy feeling that we are all in a happy routine together.

This, of course, is not real play-writing. The real writer often disturbs or shocks us because he sees the attractiveness and the fears of life more vividly. Series plays sometimes are very good indeed, but the separate single play usually offers a deeper experience. The trouble is that these plays need looking out for, and they mean taking a risk. When you tune in to a weekly series, you know roughly what will follow for the next half hour. When you tune in to a separate play, you may find that it is not to your taste. It is, however, a risk worth taking.

Looking out for plays

In the *Radio Times* and *Television Times* fairly full details are given of most plays. This is the place to choose—not the columns of the daily paper because there is not enough space there to give more than the title. The title of a play on its own does not give much idea. The fuller details of author, director, and cast give you a slightly better idea. Here for instance is the entry in the *Radio Times* for Barry Hines' *Speech Day*:

Programmes for 26 March

BBC1   **Monday tv**

Ronnie's leaving school—and perhaps a lot more—behind him: 9.25

9.25 *Colour*
Play for Today
Speech Day
by BARRY HINES
with
David Smith as Ronnie Warboys
Speech Day is a bit of a laugh if you are not one of nature's prize-winners. But now that they've finished with school and school with them, what comes next for Ronnie, Wally and Rob?
Headmaster
               JOHN FORBES-ROBERTSON
Deputy Headmaster
               GEOFF TOMLINSON
George........................BILL DEAN
Mr Warboys...........BRIAN GLOVER
Wally................KEVIN JENKINSON
Robson........................GLEN DALBY
Danny Warboys.ANDREW BEAUMONT
Mrs Warboys........ELIZABETH DAWN
Grandfather............MICHAEL ATHA
Mayor...................... JOHN ROLLS
Douglas.................TONY CAUNTER
Maths master......LEONARD FENTON
Art master..........BERNARD WRIGLEY
Sanderson.............PETER WALLIS
Professor Jessup
               WILFRED HARRISON
Miss Bedford......DENISE MOCKLER
Woodwork master..... PAUL COPLEY
PE master..........GARY MCDERMOTT
Domestic Science...MARY VAUGHAN
Film editor PETER COULSON
Film cameraman BRIAN TUFANO
Script editor ANN SCOTT
Producer GRAEME MCDONALD
Director JOHN GOLDSCHMIDT
(Barry Hines discusses his play in *Real Time*, Thursday 11.50 BBC2)

The biggest clue in these details is the name of the author. Actors and actresses are the best-known people concerned with television, and certainly a good performer is worth watching, but it is the author whose imagination and strength of feeling is of most importance. It is worth, therefore, reading the authors' names, noting those whose plays you enjoy, and looking out for them again.

Even these details though are very brief. Sometimes the *Radio Times* and *Television Times* print an introductory note to the play. Unfortunately these introductory notes are thought of as "publicity" and are often not as helpful as they might be. Still they do give some idea which will help you choose—far better than the bald title in the daily paper.

It is always interesting to compare your opinions with other people's: this you can do not only by talking to friends, but also by reading the critics in the newspapers and magazines. *The Listener* is in most school libraries and contains regular reviews of most BBC productions. The daily papers often, but not always, review television plays. A really thoughtful review deepens your enjoyment of the play. Regular reading of the television critics will also help you to get to know the better writers so that you can look out for their plays. Here is a review of another of the plays that appeared in a daily newspaper:

These are ways of helping the viewer to choose television plays in advance and to think about them afterwards. The large and varied output of adaptations from novels and stage plays and of original plays for television provides the screen of a television set with a rich repertoire of interesting plays—they are worth watching and thinking about carefully.

Questions for Discussion and Writing

Reasonable Suspicion

1 Before the scene in which Pooley and Neil meet, we are shown what they were doing just beforehand—Pooley being niggled about his job by Geoff, Neil quarrelling with his girlfriend. How do these events affect the way they behave when they meet?

2 "As long as what is loosely termed 'the human race' fouls up the pavements instead of making daisy chains, there'll always be nasty little, power-happy establishment lackeys like me asking a lot of law-abiding citizens like *you* stupid questions like *this*." (page 24)

Why does Smith call himself a "nasty little, power-happy establishment lackey"? Is it true?

3 "I should never have been brought here in the first place." (page 25)

Do you think Neil has been unfairly treated, or were the police acting reasonably in the circumstances? By the end of the play, do you think either side has understood the point of view of the other?

4 Why is Ken so angry with Pooley at the end of the play?

5 As the play ends, we see the old man who was "seen off" by Pooley at the beginning. Why do you think the author included these two scenes? For instance—would your attitude to Pooley be any different if you hadn't seen him dealing with the old man in the last shot?

6 How would *you* react if a police officer turned up and asked you questions when you hadn't done anything? How would *you* react if you were a police officer faced with a difficult character who didn't want to co-operate? Improvise a scene in pairs—have a turn at each part. Or write a piece of dialogue.

A Right Dream of Delight

7 "It's like all Fontaine's offers, you'll find there's a catch in it somewhere." (page 43)

Do you agree with Gerry's view of Fontaine? If the employees like the extras, does it matter what Fontaine's motives are for providing them?

Does it matter that there isn't a union for the workers?

Would *you* work for Fontaine? Do you think there really

are firms like this, or is it an exaggeration?

8 Gerry calls Doris a human robot, whose life is controlled by Fontaine. Doris calls Gerry a Wild Man of Borneo, and says he never wants anyone to "get on". Whom do you have most sympathy with?

Do you think the authors mean you to take them seriously as real people, or are they caricatures? If so, why?

9 Why does Madeleine despise the firm? How do her reasons differ from Gerry's?

Why does she spend so much time on Paul?

10 On page 64 Madeleine says "Don't let them hear you call it a factory, it's a production centre". And on page 76 the American has a very roundabout phrase for sacking— "effectuating a rationalisation of labour which will involve the disposal of ten per cent of the labour force."

Why do you think they use euphemisms instead of saying plainly what they mean?

Can you think of other situations where people use euphemisms? (Have a look at some political speeches, for instance.)

Try inventing some of your own: write a letter to employees from the Fontaine management telling them that the factory is going to close down.

11 What will happen to the Muddimans in the future? And what about the Walshes? Write an extra scene or scenes showing what becomes of them all.

Speech Day

12 On page 90, Miss Bedford reads the report of one of the members of 5GI:

"Shirley could do better if only she tried harder"—and she comments, "Of course she could do better if only they gave her something better to do."

The master of the Top Stream class wouldn't have agreed with her. This is *his* comment about Ronnie Warboys, who has been sent to mow the lawn (page 91):

"It's all right for him, he's nothing better to do with his time. I've got to get *you* lot through an examination at the end of next year." Whose attitude do you agree with? Should 5GI have their time filled by mowing the lawn and tidying up, or are there more important things they could do, and that the school should provide?

Are there any signs in the play that these pupils are not just "plain stupid"? What would you say were their talents? Why aren't these talents valued as highly by the school as "Speech Day" successes?

13　George and the Mayor had a similar background, but when we meet them in the play they are on very different levels of society. George feels that success has spoiled the Mayor—" . . . it finished him, Ronnie, he got respectable." (page 105)

On the other hand, the Mayor sees it like this: "As I got older I got more sense. . . . Things are not always as simple as they might first appear." (page 106)

What do you understand by these two remarks? Are you on one side or the other? Whom do you prefer as a person, George or the Mayor? Why?

14　Grandpa: "But I agree with what Lenin said, when he said we ain't interested in size of crumbs or even slices of cake. We want bakery, he said, so that we can determine the sort of cake that's to be baked."

What does this mean? Which characters in the play own "the bakery" and how do they determine the "cake"?

15　We're shown quite a lot of Ronnie Warboy's home background during the play, and we see his father and brother at work. How do you think this background affects Ronnie's attitude to school?

Write an extra scene where you show the home background of one of the Speech Day "successes". Try not to exaggerate too much—make the characters possible and real—but try too to bring out any differences that you think there might be between them and the Warboys.

16　Why does Robson's leather jacket matter so much to Mr. Sanderson? (page 96) And why do you suppose it matters to Robson?

What are your own opinions about school uniform?

17　On page 94, the boys from 5GI invent some new prizes for Speech Day.

Have a go at inventing your own Speech Day that would mean something to the whole school. Write a different speech for the headmaster, decide on who would present the prizes and what the prizes would be for (unless you decide to abolish them?) and what singing or other entertainment there would be.

It can be a joke if you like; but it might be worth thinking seriously about it too, and planning one that would really work as an alternative.

The Piano

18 Most of the main characters—Willie, Ada, Edgar, and Mabel—have their own particular obsessions over which they are very obstinate. What are these different obsessions, and can you suggest why it is that the characters find it so hard to see each other's points of view?
Why do you think that it's Ada who gives in?

19 The main story could be told without the character of Jeremy appearing at all. Why do you think the author included him?

20 Can you think of a solution to the problem which would have saved the piano? Or do you agree with Willie that "it's had its day"?

21 Although on one level this is just a story about a piano that is too big to fit in a bungalow, on another level the piano is a symbol for something much deeper. Try to explain what the piano stands for.

22 Do you think the new town Willie wants to build will be better or worse than the old one? What will be the probable losses and gains?

General Questions

23 In most of the plays in this collection, there are examples of people coming into conflict with one another because they have different interests and are unable to step into some-one else's shoes and understand *their* point of view.
Have any of the plays helped you to sympathise with some-one you might, in everyday life, simply dislike? What was it that you learned about them which made this possible?

24 The characters in these plays are under many different kinds of pressure. Which situation would *you* find hardest to bear? Could it be prevented?

25 Even though you were reading the plays instead of seeing them, you probably had a fairly strong visual impression of some of the characters.

26 Describe any one character whom you could picture clearly, and try to explain how you built this picture up.
Did you feel that any of the plays, or parts of the plays, suffered from being read and not seen?

The Authors

Richard Harris

Richard Harris is a prolific television playwright, having written over two hundred scripts. His first was "The Christmas Card" in 1959. In fact this, based on his own experiences, was also the very first play he had written. His plays have been performed on such series as *Play of the Month*, *The Wednesday Play*, and *Armchair Theatre*. He has devised four television series, and contributed scripts to other series, such as *The Avengers*, *Public Eye*, and *Hunter's Walk*, for which his play in this volume was written. He also writes stage plays, and two have been produced in the West End: *Albert and Virginia* and the comedy *Two and Two make Sex*.

Barry Hines

The son of a miner, Barry Hines was born in the village of Hoyland Common near Barnsley in 1939. As a schoolboy at Ecclesfield Grammar School he was chosen to play for the England Grammar Schools' soccer team. When he left school he played football for Barnsley, usually in the "A" team, while doing a variety of jobs including working as a labourer mending hydraulic pit props and as a blacksmith's assistant. He then trained as a PE teacher at Loughborough Training College and taught for two years in a London comprehensive school. *The Blinder* was his first novel, but he is more widely known for his second book, *A Kestrel for a Knave*, which was published in 1968 and which was turned into the highly successful film *Kes*. His play *Billy's Last Stand* is in *The Experience of Work* and there is a section from *The Blinder* included in *The Experience of Sport* (both in this series).

Julia Jones

Julia Jones writes regularly for television, but started her career as an actress. She was born in Liverpool, and towards the end of the war joined the ATS (Auxilary Territorial Service). After her demobilisation, she won a scholarship to the Royal Academy of Dramatic Art. Her first professional work was acting for Joan Littlewood's "Theatre Workshop" company in Manchester and then Stratford East. With that company she toured Czechoslovakia and Sweden. Later she acted for many years in repertory and touring companies, appearing in the

West End in Alun Owen's "Progress to the Park". She says that all this theatrical experience was "a wonderful training for a playwright".

Her first play for television was "The Navigators" in 1965, and since then she has written both plays of her own (such as "Back of Beyond") and adaptations (such as "Anne of Green Gables"). Her play "Devon Violets" won the first prize in the Prague Television Festival in 1970. More recently she has written stage plays also, including "The Garden".

Jeremy Seabrook and Michael O'Neill

Both authors went to Northampton Grammar School and from there to Cambridge University, where Jeremy Seabrook studied languages and Michael O'Neill anthropology. Jeremy Seabrook taught for some years in Northampton, and then went on to the London School of Economics to take a Diploma in Social Administration, and worked as a Social Worker. Michael O'Neill went to America for two years, and when he returned became a teacher.

Together they have written nineteen plays. Jeremy Seabrook on his own has written two books *The Underprivileged* and *City Close-up*. The plays and the books explore in a variety of ways the problems of modern urban life.

Other Television plays in this Series

Whether for reading as plays in their own right or as part of television study courses, the other collections of television plays in this series are likely to be of interest to readers of this volume:

Conflicting Generations
    scripts by John Hopkins, Paddy Chayefsky, David Turner, Ronald Eyre, and John Mortimer

Scene Scripts
    from the BBC schools television series, scripts by Bill Lyons, Alan Plater, Rex Edwards, Michael Cahill, Ronald Eyre, Fay Weldon, and Keith Dewhurst, with an introduction on television production by Ronald Smedley

Scene Scripts Two
    a second selection from the series

Steptoe and Son
    a selection of Ray Galton and Alan Simpson's original scripts for the famous series

Z Cars
    a selection by Keith Dewhurst, Ronald Eyre, John Hopkins, and Alan Plater

Softly, Softly
    a selection by Elwyn Jones, the originator of the series, of five of his own scripts

Watt's Progress
    a selection by Elwyn Jones, of scripts from *Z Cars* through to *Softly, Softly* exploring the character of John Watt, and showing his promotion and the main stages in his life

Television Scripts in Schools

Like its companion collection, *Conflicting Generations*, this book is a collection of television plays selected for reading with older groups in secondary schools with two aims in mind: Firstly, to provide a collection of good *plays* that are worth reading carefully and have themes that are worth pondering. Secondly, to gather examples of television scripts that can be used to give a firm basis for topical discussions on the fleeting art of television. Each of these plays was a notable success when it was produced on television.

Many of the most worthwhile dramatists of the present time have written some of their best work for television, and the very limitations of television drama—the need for compression—in many ways help classroom reading. The theme is necessarily compressed and pupils can retain the whole of the play in their minds. This particular selection has been chosen to offer variety of atmosphere, range of characters, and contrasts of approach. At the same time, however, the plays have been brought together because the themes and dramatic moments link in a way that is likely to appeal and have significance for the readers in the fourth years and above in secondary schools. The title, introductory note, and questions have been devised to point the comparisons and echoes that, I hope, give the collection a unity.

Schools have wanted for many years to bring the experience of television into the creative critical discussion of the classroom. Many schools have devised screen appreciation courses within which this can be done; the Society for Education through Film and Television has worked to advise and make suggestions. The Newsom Report (*Half Our Future*, HMSO, 1963) confirmed the responsibility of schools:

"We should wish to add a strong claim for the study of film and television in their own right."

Twelve years later, the Bullock Report (*A Language for Life*, HMSO, 1975) pleaded even more strongly that schools should make work in film and especially television a normal part of their study. It is worth noting the main points that the report made in this respect (paragraph 22.14):

"One of the most powerful sources of vivid experience is the general output programmes of television, particularly documentaries and drama. Many teachers are already basing a good deal of classroom work on such programmes. In some primary

172

schools they use after-school programmes as a stimulus for talking and writing, and assemble collections of books to exploit the interest the programmes arouse. In secondary schools the practice is more widespread, and we met teachers who brought the experience of the television screen into the classroom, preparing for evening programmes and following them up the next day. Some classes were reading the texts of television plays with enjoyment and others were writing scenes for themselves. In a few schools we came across serious study of the medium of television itself. We were impressed by such work as we did see but are concerned that a decade after the publication of the Newsom Report there is still little evidence of the kind of study it recommended. . . . We believe that in relation to English there is a case for the view that a school should use it not as an aid but as a disseminator of experience. In this spirit we recommend an extension of this work. Although there is unquestioned value in developing a critical approach to television, as to listening and reading, we would place the emphasis on extending and deepening the pupils' appreciation. This could be achieved by three complementary approaches:

(a) the group study of television programmes, extracts, and scripts alongside other media dealing with the same theme;

(b) the study of a full-length television work in its own right, with associated discussion and writing;

(c) the study of television as a medium, with some exploration of production methods, comparison with other media, and analysis of the output of programmes.

In addition to home viewing such activities would involve the playback in school hours of video-recorded evening programmes, and some reading of the literature of television."

Imprint Books have made a consistent effort to meet this need by a complementary collection of volumes of television scripts (listed on page 176), and it is hoped that *The Pressures of Life* will be especially valuable, exploring as it does many aspects of contemporary society. The section *Thinking about Television Plays* has been included as a way of broadening the discussion from these particular plays to the whole subject of television drama.

In this discussion the emphasis has been deliberately placed on *content*, but at the same time I hope the pupils' attention is drawn to the televisual presentation in some detail. A danger of television study in schools is that the wonders of television technique will become more important than the artistic purpose to which those techniques are used. "Professional presentation" is a meaningless decoration unless it serves imaginative writing. No amount of analysis of camera and editing technique is a substitute for involved discussion of what the play is about. On the other hand, classroom discussion should always be well grounded in the actual text, and the plays should not be used as the merest springboard for a free-wheeling discussion of "old age" or "attitudes towards authority". This volume will be found most effective if the reading, writing, and talking engendered by it is firmly focussed on the actual plays.

M.M.

Acknowledgements

We are grateful to the following for permission to include these plays which are in copyright:

ATV Network Limited who produced the series, *Hunter's Walk* and Ted Willis who created the series, author, and author's agent, Harvey Unna and Stephen Durbridge Limited, 14 Beaumont Mews, Marylebone High Street, London W1N 4HE, for the play *Reasonable Suspicion* by Richard Harris from the *Hunter's Walk* series; the author and author's spokesman, Curtis Brown Limited, 1 Craven Hill, London W2 3EP, for *Speech Day* by Barry Hines; the author and author's agent, Fraser and Dunlop Scripts Limited, 91 Regent Street, London W1R 8RU, for *The Piano* by Julia Jones; the authors and authors' agent, Clive Goodwin Associates, 79 Cromwell Road, London SW7 5BN, for *A Right Dream of Delight* (formerly *A State of Welfare*) by Jeremy Seabrook and Michael O'Neill.

We wish to thank the following for permission to reproduce photographs:

Associated Television Corporation Ltd., page 2 (top and bottom) and cover (bottom); British Broadcasting Corporation, pages 84, 97, 108, 162 and cover (top); Noeline Kelly, page 38; The Times, page 108.

174